BEYOND THE WHITE PICKET FENCE

TRACY GROMEN

Copyright © 2021 by Tracy Gromen

ISBN13: 978-1-913728-58-8

All rights reserved.

No part of this book may be reproduced in any form or by any electronic or mechanical means, including information storage and retrieval systems, without written permission from the author, except for the use of brief quotations in a book review.

DEDICATION

To my husband, Luke - Thank you for loving me EXACTLY as I am and going on this journey with me. Your grounded, loving strength has carried me more times than you will ever know. I learn from your love every single minute of every day. Thank you for creating a loving partnership with me. I love you Always and Forever.

To my sons, Gavin, Connor and Brennan - Thank you for showing me what unconditional love looks and feels like. You are forever my why and you have been my greatest teachers. Being your mom IS one of my childhood dreams realized. My life is so much richer with you being in it. Thank you for sharing your light with me AND with the world. I am forever grateful. I love you to the moon and back.

To my parents, Kathy and Gordon McGinnis - Thank you for loving me the best way that you know how. Thank you for teaching me the best way that you know how. Thank you for growing with me. Thank you for helping me become exactly who I am today. You are the perfect parents for me. You helped me build my life today - and it is SO much better than the "white picket fence life" that I wished for when I was a kid. I love you very much.

To my friends, Thank you for thinking that my "weirdness" is awesome.

To my experiences, Thank you for helping me to grow and for shaping who I am today.

To God, Thank you for loving me and supporting me unconditionally no matter what, exactly as I am, even through all the times that my wounds wanted to dispute your unconditional love for me. Thank you for honoring my free will and choice, allowing me to take all of the time that I needed to connect to you in my heart in a way that felt good and safe for me. I commit myself and my healing gifts to you.

To you, Thank you for being here and reading my book. Thank you for DECIDING that it's your time to create a life that you want by healing your wounds, turning them into wisdom and freeing yourself from the baggage of invisible "white picket fence" emotional pain.

I am a person that matters because I am.

And so are you.

CONTENTS

Disclaimer — vii
My Promise To You — ix
Introduction — xii

1. ALL of my clients are psychic and intuitive — 1
2. Doing what is right for your soul — 15
3. Your Own Little Devil — 34
4. Healing Your Lucy — 64
5. Taking Lucy out of the driver's seat and re-discover your power — 80
6. Gaining perspective is the balm that soothes Lucy AND moves you forward — 98
7. Heart Cojones — 118
8. Pedestals and crosses — 138

Afterword — 159
References — 167
About the Author — 169

DISCLAIMER

This book is a self-help book. Through the exercises, you might experience triggering emotions. Sometimes those triggers don't feel good, but you are safe no matter what. This is why I have included exercises intended for self-healing such as letter writing and tapping. Some of the exercises involve hypnosis, which is being put into a deeply relaxed hypnotic state. If you have epilepsy or a psychotic illness, you should not go into hypnosis.

If you choose to continue with the book, the exercises and the downloadable hypnosis sessions, you are accepting full responsibility for taking part in the exercises, tapping, hypnosis and agreeing that Tracy Gromen or SoulHeartedly Happy, LLC holds no liability for any potential outcome.

Also, I am not a medical doctor, licensed therapist, counselor or social worker. I do not purport to diagnose, treat or cure any illness. If you are currently under medical treatment, please consult your medical provider if you have any questions regarding your condition.

This is a self-help book, which includes self-help healing sessions - you take full responsibility for any outcomes that you create as a result of participating in this book/the exercises/hypnosis session.

Thanks for being here! I appreciate you!

MY PROMISE TO YOU

If you commit to this practice and implement the steps in this book, your life will shift in a positive direction. You will feel more at peace with yourself and that will allow your life to feel richer and fuller.

If you build conviction in WHY your healing is important for YOU - and implement what I share in this book - you will grow to appreciate all parts of yourself more and more everyday. You will give yourself the emotional nourishment that you have been seeking outside of yourself. And that is what builds satisfaction and centeredness in your life.

When you feel your light within you - on purpose, you will feel more complete and more whole.

Create a life that feels present and complete, by your success standards.

One decision at a time.

Your healing IS the impact that you have been searching for.

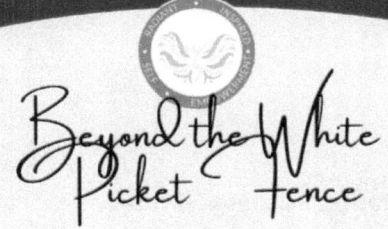

"Yesterday I was clever, so I wanted to change the world. Today I am wise, so I am changing myself."

~Rumi

INTRODUCTION

SAGGY BOOBS

"Are your boobs gonna be saggy, mom?"

That was the question that my son asked and thank God that he did because it broke up ALL of the tension and seriousness of the moment. Whenever I call my boys down to the kitchen table for a family meeting, the question they always ask is, "Did somebody die?" So as they bounded down the stairs from their rooms and took a seat at the table, question upon question began firing.

"Did someone die?"

"Is everything okay?"

"Why are we here?"

I just smiled, welcomed them to sit and let the energy settle.

I began the conversation by answering all the above questions, "No, nobody's died; yes, everything is okay and I am going to tell you why you are here. Have a seat so I can talk to you."

INTRODUCTION

A hush fell over the table because my boys DO know that when I call them down to a family meeting, there IS something to say.

It wasn't just my three sons at the table. My middle son's girlfriend joined too. She wasn't going to at first - I looked at her and said, "You've been in this family for a number of years now, so stay." I chuckled and said, "You will find out within the next ten minutes anyway and he will need your support."

I had no idea how nervous I would be. I took a deep breath, gathered up my energy and began speaking. "On June 21st I'm going into surgery to have my breast implants removed. No, nothing is wrong that I know of, but back in 2019 I got an intuitive hit that said it was time for them to come out. I was planning on getting them out last year and then Covid happened. It's okay if you are angry at me or scared or anything - you can come to me or you can go to your dad or you can talk to each other, just know that I love you, your feelings are normal and I am willing to experience all of them."

There was a quiet I'd never experienced. We are a LOUD family so this degree of quiet was a combination of deep fear and deep reverence for the moment of all of us being together.

God, they looked as scared as I felt.

Then the tension broke. My son asked as he wrinkled his nose, "So, not that I really want to know about your boobs, but will they be saggy?"

We laughed. That breath of fresh air of laughter.

No, they would not be saggy.

Then my other son chimed in, 'So, you will be like a penguin for a bit?"

INTRODUCTION

Again, laughter rang through the air. "Yes, I won't be able to lift my arms for fourteen days, so more like a T-Rex."

I looked each of them in the eye and said, "My intuition is always right, I trust my doctor. I am in the best shape for this surgery. I trust that I will be safe. And yes, I will need your help."

It was one of the most uncomfortable conversations that I have ever had. Not because I felt badly about the decision that I'd made, though. See, there are people who think I should have regretted having implants in the first place and I don't. I don't feel any shame for getting those breast implants and I don't feel any shame for being willing to admit that removing them was hard because I was attached to the way that they made me feel.

I searched in their eyes and realized that they were understanding to the best of their capability.

Yet they would never know what it's like to be a 46-year-old woman. They would never know what it's like to rely on your beauty as you move in this world. They would never know what it's like to struggle with the ageing process right now. Sure, they would have their own midlife issues and they would appear in individual ways and their own lives, but how could I expect them to understand what I had navigated in my life?

This didn't come from a place of victimhood, simply from a place of, "I was raised to rely on my looks," and I attached to that identity hard.

It was an important homecoming, because in their fear and in their search to understand is where I required nothing of them. I didn't require them to understand me or absolve me from any decisions I had made. I met them with acceptance of myself and honesty for where we were in that moment and I met them with

INTRODUCTION

acceptance of every emotion that they were willing to experience or run from.

For the next few weeks, each one of my boys would sit down with me and I would check in with them and sometimes they would tell me that they were fine and sometimes they would have questions about whether or not I was scared. I met them with as much honesty as I could without making them feel like they had to carry my burden.

At one point my oldest son said to me, "You seem like you are doing fine."

My answer to him was, "There are times where I get afraid and that's my work to do and the person I'm going to share that level of fear with is your father, not you. Not because I don't respect you or think that you can't handle it, but because it's not your responsibility to manage.

There was not one moment that I was sorry for getting my breast implants put in. I loved them, up until the moment that I got them out - I loved them and the way that they made me feel.

Sexy. Vibrant.

And I liked the way that my chest filled out a dress.

My husband has said before that he is sorry that I got them put in. I 100% disagree.

I never got them in for him, I got them in for myself and that's the reason I'm not sorry. I have zero shame around either decision. And that is the reason that I had this conversation alone with my boys. I wanted them to know that I harbor no shame or judgment towards my past self for getting these implants in. I wanted them to know that I trust myself fully and ALL of the decisions that I have made to get them removed.

And I wanted to give them the space to feel anything they wanted to feel from the time that I told them to the date of surgery and beyond.

My goal is to always be clear and transparent with myself and with them so that I can hold space for all of the feelings to come up on this journey of growth.

These implants gave me an opportunity to become the person that feels vibrant and sexy; to become the person that continued on her inner healing Journey to maintain a field of vibrancy, sexiness, and self-acceptance. This provided me the strength to let go of these implants.

My breast implants were like water wings.

Did I just really compare implants to water wings? - I DID! And I love the analogy.

Of course, getting them out will provide its challenges - and I am ready for them. To become MORE of myself - unapologetically.

Getting these implants out is me releasing an old identity. An identity that I just don't need anymore because I can provide it for myself from within.

I'd had my breasts implants put in back in 2007. When I made the decision in 2007 to have them put in, I did not really consider what having them removed would even look or feel like (because I did not plan on removing them - EVER!). I never even considered sitting around a table with the people that I loved the most telling them that I am going into a major surgery to undo a decision that I had made 14 years ago (one of the MOST uncomfortable conversations of my life to date). While I looked at my sons sitting around the table, I realized that in 2007 I hadn't had the appreciation for myself that I had in that moment staring into their eyes. I DO appreciate my past wounded self for navigating her feelings the best way that she knew how. I DO appreciate my wise, loving healed Self from being able to embody wisdom, grace and acceptance as she navigates this current decision. No regrets. No shame. No blame.

I thought that I would have been met with anger and that maybe somebody would have left the table.

What I was met with was stability, safety to be myself, and Trust that my relationships are durable and willing to experience hard conversations.

Yes, there was fear and there was grief, and wrapped up in that was palpable love. Palpable support. Unwavering honesty.

A reflection of what I have been creating in my life and relationships since 2011.

And maybe even before that...

This is a story of rebirth, renewal and re-discovery. Because we ALL have a second act and if you are reading this, yours has already begun.

INTRODUCTION

In the next chapter...

My parents had 'THE talk' with me when I was four years old.

"Tracy, You MUST not talk about this anymore, people will think that you're weird. STOP! Do not mention it again."

The topic?

I saw a demon in the church, got scared and told the teacher. They called my parents. Everyone was scared. I mean, why the fuck would a demon be in church? (There's a whole other story about that, but it's for another day!)

I got in trouble.

And I was also labeled 'weird'. A part of me went inside a box that day, not feeling safe to be myself because I believed them. I believed that I had done something wrong and began measuring my words. It would continue to be a skill that I held very close to me - I admitted nothing for the fear of being weird.

It was that way throughout most of my life.

That skill? Being psychic.

Do you know how much energy went into hiding this God-given ability? To hide myself and my Truth?

A lot.

When my dad died, the lid on the box flew off.

There were dead people all over the place. I'm talking *Sixth Sense*. It. Was. Bananas! And it was scary and because my inner four-year-old self was still clinging to the notion that it was wrong, I suffered and tried every which way to just make it go away -

drinking, exercise, more doing. Anything just to get out of my head and body. It was my way of closing the lid to that box.

The box got me in so much trouble. I tried to push it away for a long time and when it got to be too much, I came to the understanding that these gifts were no longer able to be hidden. I decided to slowly reintegrate this part of myself into my world.

I began to Re-Discover the safety within and around to speak and be my Truth.

I had to re-learn how to manage this skill.

And I had to learn not feel weird about it anymore. Not to feel weird about myself anymore.

Now I can say,

"Hi, I'm Tracy. I see angels, dead people, can see and exorcise demons and read energy like a badass. I also run businesses, am mom to three boys and am married to a beautiful man. I love to work out and drink wine."

I'm basically the total package.

And so are YOU!

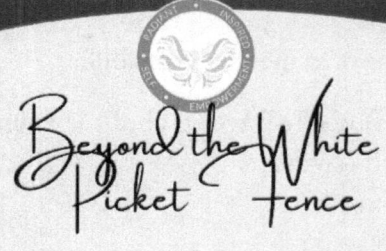

Beyond the White Picket Fence

YOU ARE UNDERGOING THE PROCESS OF REMEMBERING WHO YOU ARE.

ALL OF MY CLIENTS ARE PSYCHIC AND INTUITIVE

A young girl stands in her room, hoping that how she looks is going to bring her a good day. Is her hair done the right way? Does the outfit she picked out mean that she would be included? She quietly remembers that she didn't even pick out this outfit. Someone else did. She's not even sure why she's wearing it. She would like to wear something with a little more color or more of a pattern, but good girls don't question. They just don't question. Until about thirty years later.

It took a long time to embrace ALL of me.

Inner healing helped me welcome that part back home. The result? Wholeness. A feeling that I hadn't felt in a long time.

Here's the truth. ALL of my clients are psychic and intuitive. ALL of my clients are mystics. ALL of my clients are healers.

And 75% of their battle is removing the label of "weird".

I help moms over forty strip the weird label from those skills so that they can proudly flow freely in their life, managed in a way that's good for them.

My clients walk in all areas of business. They are thought leaders. They are Change makers.

And they KNOW how to heal themselves, to trust their intuition and use their psychic abilities.

Which fuels the confidence from within to speak their Truth instead of shutting parts of themselves away to make other people feel comfortable.

Maybe you were thinking to yourself, "Tracy, being psychic is not my gift." I bet you have something about yourself that you have been hiding because someone in the past told you that you were too much, that it was too much and that you needed to stop being so much of that.

It's time to bring that gift back home - to yourself.

Running from it is what is keeping you overwhelmed and exhausted in your life.

I used to think that I grew up a magical child born to non-magical parents. Looking back, I don't think that my parents were non-magical. I just don't think that their powers were unveiled. They weren't safe to ever experience their Magic. My grandparents didn't have the capacity to allow individual Magic within each person in the family. There were roles that you had and you did not deviate from those roles.

I remember growing up my father would make fun of my mother's side of the family, calling them a bunch of gypsies. We all laughed, but I don't think we truly understood the Magic that was available to each of us. My father's side of the family was just as magical and all of it remained unspoken. I wonder if my parents remember the day that they shut down their own Magic. I never asked.

What I knew was that I had a role to fulfill, although having a prophetic four-year-old was more than likely really scary to experience for my non-practicing magical parents. I could see things that other people didn't see and I readily said it out loud. Not knowing any better, I would speak truths that were important to be said out loud because if it was not said out loud somebody would get hurt.

Yet I was met with punishment for speaking up because it wasn't appropriate to say things about adults that were uncomfortable. Part of my Magic is being able to see the energy lines of Truth and realities that it will produce. Another part of my Magic is being an intense radar for understanding who and what is dangerous.

I spoke up for the first years of my life until I started learning that it was so much safer to not be magical in this world. It was so much safer NOT to speak my Truth because when I spoke my Truth, I got in trouble. When I was speaking in Truth, I was punished, I was shamed, I was judged. I began shutting down those gifts, although I still used them for my own benefit. And thank God that I did, because it helped me navigate and get out of some of the most dangerous situations in my childhood and which I had to heal from as an adult.

My parents were great people, yet when I was growing up they lacked in the area of providing steady emotional nourishment and support. They didn't know how to navigate their own emotions. In my household, it was either happy or there was some sort of blow-up happening. Having intense emotions was not something that was talked about back then and no one knew how to normalize the full spectrum of emotions. Because of that, no one knew how to navigate it. Since I did not have emotional nourishment and support in my house, what I found was that I received praise when I was helpful and when I achieved things. That made them happy, reduced the yelling and seemed to make my life feel less chaotic and easier.

It felt good to be needed and it felt good to be praised, which fuelled the birth of a high achiever and a people pleaser. I would spend most of my life doing those two things in order to fill up my emotional tank, because that's all I knew that produced results of feeling good and of reducing that feeling of chaos in my life. I did that for a very, very long time and it became like heroin. The need got more frequent and I began overworking, exhausting myself trying to find ways to ease my anxiety by making other people happy through constant and excessive doing. That behavior worked out really well for me until about 2006.

When things started rumbling a little bit differently in my life, I felt more anxious and had a hard time controlling it. On paper my life looked awesome - I was married to a fantastic man, I was a mom to three beautiful boys. We had everything that you'd ever want - all of our physical and material needs were met, yet I was still feeling so isolated in my own life, so lost and empty. The hardest part about feeling that was there was no logical explanation. According to the standards that I had been living by, there was no reason for me to feel so sad, lost or empty. So from 2006 until 2009 when my father passed away, I simply ran from it and judged myself profusely for not being more grateful in my life.

When my father passed away, though, it was like a lightning bolt struck into my life. I found him that morning; he died of a heart attack. In that moment of finding him, all of my Magic came back. In that moment, every emotion that I had shoved away throughout my life came crashing down. Now I would spend my time running from that for ANOTHER year and a half - I would drink; I would work out; I was a fitness instructor at that time and I used it to my advantage. I was able to drown out all of my intense emotions under the guise of needing to take on another class.

I ran away from all of the thoughts and feelings in my head and my body. Because of that, I started getting really sick on a monthly basis, which always put me on a round of antibiotics and a round of steroids. By month seven, it was clear that something was wrong since I was not getting better. I just kept on repeating the same cycle OVER and OVER again. I had two weeks of intense working and then getting sick for two weeks. I finally went to seek traditional medicine. I looked fine, but I did not feel fine. I couldn't shake this illness and I couldn't shake the underlying feeling of being lost in my life.

When I was "healthy", I showed up with what I refer to now as fake confidence. It was the sort of confidence in which I would perform in my life, keep everybody happy, and really hide from myself. I was showing up as a 150-watt bulb only to fall back into feeling even more empty by the end of the day. Admitting that to myself felt raw and vulnerable and I did not like it – so I would go back to performing and just doing things to get away from it.

I didn't know how to navigate this. I went through all of this medical testing to begin figuring out what was wrong with me. There were so many tests, so many potential diagnoses and then the doctor came back and said, "Your immune system isn't working properly, so we are going to spark your immune system by giving you some immunizations to jump start your system. In a week, you're going to be fine." I clapped my hands together in delight, got the shots and headed out the door to go home.

I got REALLY sick that weekend, so much so that I got a little frightened. I thought to myself, "Well, I need to get better and this is that pathway, so it's fine." Something inside of me rumbled again, though. It wasn't fine. There was a message that I was missing - again. I got a call two weeks later to say that all of the treatments and shots had worked, my blood work was normal and I was good to go.

Hot damn! Woohoo! I felt free, walked a little taller and began to resume my "normal" life.

Exactly two weeks later, I turned gray. All of a sudden I couldn't walk up the stairs. I had gone from teaching four classes a day to not being able to walk up the stairs. I got scared for the first time in my life because I could feel my life-force energy leaving me. It was the weirdest sensation and it was the fire alarm that finally got my attention.

It wasn't the nine months of being ill that got my attention nor the year prior of rolling around in excessive guilt and anger and self-hatred, not only over my dad's passing, but over my life, over all of the times that I was shut down, over all the times that I was ignored. Over all the times I had to hide my Magic. So I went to bed with the last round of antibiotics that I promised my doctor I would go on. I went on this round of antibiotics, and I fell asleep. And what I had then was the most deep and profound mystical experience.

I would call myself a high achieving badass and I know that I can create anything that I want to create. And I'm also magical. There is a difference in who I am now compared to who I was then. A person without their magic activated is a high achieving badass hustling for all of their worth. That was me. During that time, my Magic would appear in fits and starts. When it did, the old wounds would fire up, telling me that it was unsafe to say the things that I needed to admit in my life, to finally acknowledge the things that were not working anymore.

This mystical experience during my time in bed was similar to an Ebenezer Scrooge moment. I was shown my life - past, present and two futures. I was shown a fork in the road. The fork in the road pointed to a very clear result if I decided to stay on this path because what I had been doing was abusing myself with my behavior. If I decided to stay on this path of self-abuse, of ignoring my own needs and failing to make necessary changes in my life, I was going to die.

This experience was so profound, so clear, so REAL and it scared the shit out of me.

Then this other pathway appeared. At the end of this pathway was a sign that said: *renewed and restored health*. That's all it said. I thought to myself," Fuck, yeah, I'm going there!" It was the obvious choice. So I began navigating down that path. I had no idea what was on that path. All I knew was that I didn't want to leave my boys or my husband. For the first time in a long time, I valued this life that I had been living even though up it had felt isolating, lonely and empty.

I wanted to stay here. I never wanted anything so much.

My life mattered. I mattered. And it was time to choose me. In doing so, I would be around for my family. As a child, my parents divorced and for a while I had an experience of my mother leaving me. She got together with somebody that beat her so badly she nearly died. The psychological damage that she suffered caused her to actually to really go away for a while. After that beating, it took her about two years to come back. I missed out on at least three years of a connection with my mother because of that. I didn't want my boys to have the experience of not having a powerful mother in their life.

I got up after those three days sleeping in bed, out of that mystical experience and got cracking to create a different movement in my life. I've created some fantastic new results in my life. And it started with just following little intuitive hits one by one. I started changing my diet. During this time since 2011, I have gone gluten- and dairy-free. I have researched vaccine injury and been able to make some new choices on that in my life and for my kids. I have become an energy healer, which means I have experienced all of the different modalities of healing.

It was in following all of these intuitive hits to rebuild myself that unshakable confidence from within was birthed. Here's the reason why. I was more than okay with it even when those around me thought otherwise. Everybody around me thought I was batshit crazy for making the changes that I made, exploring the things that I explored. I'm in the Midwest, in a rural area outside of Cleveland, Ohio, USA. It's basically meat, potatoes, God, guns and hard work.

These people are some of the greatest people that you will meet. Handshakes still matter and integrity is everything. Back then, though, you didn't talk about having mystical experiences and you sure as shit didn't start moving in your life in a way that was different from the pack without getting some strong pressure to retreat into the "pack" mind.

The pack mind has a specific plan of what a good life looks like - what I call the "white picket fence" life. The plan that our parents and those people around us set forth - go to college, get a job (it doesn't matter if you like it or not), get married, raise a family. This plan forgot one essential ingredient - your own life satisfaction and fulfillment on your own terms and taking the time to ask yourself more questions about what YOU want (and being okay with that even when it is different from the pack).

I DID leave the pack mind, though, because my life depended on it. That meant that I had to go through this willingness to navigate what it felt like to leave the tribe. Some of this work, a lot of this work, feels lonely at times. It is the reason that I am so passionate about helping women navigate their transformation. Because it feels fucking scary to do so. Your family will look at you like you're batshit crazy. Mine did.

Back when I began my own inner healing journey in 2011, there was no gluten- and dairy-free eating, unless you were in the posh cities like New York City, Los Angeles and Miami. In Cleveland, Ohio, eating dairy-free or gluten-free was the mark of a weirdo. A hippie. I found myself doing research and implementing it sort of secretly until I developed the inner safety within to not give so many fucks about what they thought, and to be able to shepherd that part of myself that cared, home to my own heart for healing.

It's never the side eyes and the deep sighs that we get from strangers that rattle our cages of shame and self-judgment. I mean really, who gives a fuck about them or what they think. It's when our spouses look at us like we're crazy or our parents question what we are doing or our kids are embarrassed to share the lunch that they have packed full of GF and DF goodness, or our best friends begin to not invite us to coffee that leaves us questioning ourself.

Is leaving the pack mind worth the effort or is it just easier to go along with the pack programming?

I got tired of shoving away the inner chaos in order to fit in. And inner healing helped me not only reduce that, it allowed me to shine a bit brighter day by day, which created a great ripple of transformation in my life.

Yes, going on the pathway of self-transformation IS worth it. I know that everyone around me thought I was crazy and it felt like icky uncomfortableness to do this work knowing that the people I love the most thought I was losing it. What I had within me was a clear vision, the image of that fork in the road of the choices available to me AND the potential outcomes.

**I LEFT THE PACK MIND -
I DID NOT LEAVE THE PACK.**

Exactly ten years later as I write this book, what I have learned along the pathway is that what I now feel from within is what I had been looking for my whole life. That part of me that I had boxed away has not only been reintegrated into myself, I have expanded all of those parts and stepped into the greatest level of centered, unshakable confidence than I've ever known.

Most of those people around me have re-discovered parts of themselves and have found an openness within themselves to try new things (some are even gluten- and dairy-free now), all because I maintained the vision that I held for renewed and restored health, which DID happen. I am free from all of my health issues and for the past ten years have only been in the doctor's office for an annual well visit.

I have so much more than that, though. I have a blend of logic and love that partner together to create unparalleled wisdom that I get to share with those who have the eyes to see, the ears to hear and the determination to navigate all parts of the inner healing path.

The white picket fence life is a life built on someone else's plan and expectations. A life that is built by what the pack deems "normal" and "fulfilling". It is in this space that you will always be chasing for more as a means to satisfy and fulfill you instead of deciding for yourself what YOU want, free from the pack plan and the pack expectations. When you feel the rumble and hear the call, you are being called to create a life that is specific to you. It is where you go BEYOND the white picket fence. To open and re-discover your own Magic within and around you.

You are ready; let's go!

∽

✨ Go Beyond the White Picket Fence Exercise ✨

Download the Free Workbook to access the 3-minute Feel Safe Now audio

https://gromen.lpages.co/beyond-the-white-picket-fence-workbook/

In the next chapter...

In 2011, I was known for hiding myself away.

It was really frustrating because I was trying my hardest to create calm in my life along with moving forward in my business. And trying to do so from a place of confidence.

And it wasn't working because I was breaking myself down believing everyone else's doubt AND believing my own. Layers and layers of shame and judgment seemed to swallow me whole as I secretly bashed myself for not feeling more confident in myself.

I believed in my goals, right? So what the fuck was the problem?

Not being able to figure out HOW to be confident and stay that way made me feel like a total failure. Which I hated...

It made me feel Hollow. Defeated. Secretly Pissed.

So I would wait for the moments that I DID feel confident to move forward. and that created loads of stopping and starting in my life and in my business.

What I wanted was to feel safe to move forward and good within myself as I did. For the longest time, I searched for support from everyone outside of me only to scrutinize whether or not it was "real". I spent time trying to find it from them until I finally realized that they could not give me what I was refusing to find from within.

And so I turned to the only person who could actually create more confidence in my life and business... me. Then I could lower that hyper nervous system that always seemed to fire when I was just trying to be more of myself.

THE SECRETS TO YOUR MAGIC AND RE-DISCOVERING IT ARE BURIED WITHIN YOU. IT IS IN YOUR HEALING THAT YOUR TRUE CONFIDENCE IS UNLEASHED

DOING WHAT IS RIGHT FOR YOUR SOUL

Once upon a time there was a girl that just wanted to feel better on the inside instead of being filled with doubt and uncertainty. She was convinced that if she just got rid of those feelings, then she would be free to be bold... confident... *more* of herself, no matter what anyone else thought.

After many years of chasing other people's ideas about how to be more confident, she stopped and looked in the place she had never thought she'd find it - buried deep within.

I walked my new pathway emotionally alone for a long while.

It was slow. And daunting. I ran into all kinds of mind drama and through it - I persisted because I wanted the result so badly.

And I made a promise to myself to make it easier for other women navigating the desire to create calm for themselves.

To create higher levels of unshakable confidence from within instead of waiting for the confidence to show up or donning a persona that exudes this glowing confidence - when on the inside it feels nothing of the sort.

Fake confidence is an illusion. The term "fake it until you make it" can be so crippling. Many of the women that I work with would be categorized as some of the most confident women out there. They can hold their own in a boardroom and have created a lot of success for themselves. Yet when they are alone in the deepest parts of their minds, they STILL feel uncertain and unworthy in different areas of their life. It keeps them running and hustling for their worth in ways that are simply unhealthy.

It is what keeps them from connecting to themselves and to others.

It is what keeps them doing and giving so much. Being everything to everyone. Sacrificing themselves over and over again, letting that wounded part of them run the show of their life from the subconscious realm.

We begin working together to help them re-discover their unshakeable confidence. That part of them that knows what they want and what they don't want so that they can heal the shame and judgment that tells them that they are "a bad person" or "not a good mom/wife/entrepreneur", which allows them to begin to take the steps to become more whole instead of doing for validation and praise.

Confidence is not only the lion's roar. It's the part of you that also says, I am willing to feel the ick and do what is right for my soul.

Unshakeable confidence is who you are and how you are willing to pick yourself up even when you are shaking on the inside, knowing that you need to move forward WHILE you feel so wobbly around it. Most of us were raised that when you feel good, you are on the right pathway and that when you feel bad, something is wrong.

And that whole concept is untrue.

To be more of who you are unapologetically, you must develop a willingness to dance with the four shadow pillars of growth. When you do, you begin to let go of these old beliefs that you shouldn't ever experience a "bad" feeling. You let go of the belief that it is wrong to prioritize yourself and take care of your needs. You begin to trust those people around you to take care of themselves so that you can point your energy towards your own growth.

These four shadow pillars, when navigated through the lens of growth, build more resilience and self-compassion from within.

The four shadow pillars are: doubt, unworthiness, misalignment, and betrayal.

It spells 'dumb'. I did that on purpose because when the shadow pillars are activating in our lives and we believe them, we make decisions that in the long run will have us judging ourselves for being dumb. You're not dumb at all, you just hit the shadow pillars and didn't know how to plan for and navigate them. Instead, you judged them, resisted yourself for feeling them and you shamed them, which led you to put them back in that tight little box. When you did this, you retreated from yourself instead of meeting your own side eyes in deep sighs.

Retreating from experiencing these pillars is what keeps you looking for validation from other people around you. Whenever I did this, I ended up finding people that held the same fearful beliefs that I was having and talking to them just talked me out of my own vision.

Every single thing that we experience from another person and their opinion is really just the vibration of these pillars activating. Then we layer on the shame and self-judgment of thinking that we shouldn't be experiencing this level of intense emotion at the age we are.

I remember asking myself what was wrong with me. Why couldn't I move through this? I actually thought that it was wrong that I was even experiencing any of this and because it felt so wrong, I always ended up turning away until my back was against the wall and I needed to make a new decision.

I needed to decide to leave the pack mind and create my own life according to my own success standards. Your unshakable confidence is developed by meeting these pillars over and over again. By having a willingness to experience all of the emotions, no matter what, on the journey. Because when you open yourself up to the availability of experiencing these intense emotions, you develop a greater level of inner safety and resilience from within. Instead of waiting for the people around you to soothe you or to agree with you or to give you permission to move forward, you do so from your own internal will to create something that is right for you - to really embrace and amplify your uniqueness and how you want to live and interact in this world.

It is the inner safety that you have and the vision that you hold that allow you to move forward, even when your family thinks you're nuts. My family thought that I was joining a cult - THEY DID! Looking back on it, it was actually one of the most comical things ever. I saw their fear of me leaving the pack.

In all of the work that I have done personally and professionally with other women, it's not the shadow pillars that are the biggest issue. It's this shame and the judgment that we experience for having them.

Because there's a part of our wounded ego (that part of our wounded selves) that thinks we shouldn't have to experience it. That thinks we are entitled to experience something easier. That part doesn't know how to fail (and does not want to learn). I had to learn how to fail. In this new realm, in the pathway to renewed and restored health, what I had to do was understand where I was resisting the shadow pillars - and WHY.

It is the shadow pillars that hold the gold - the wisdom that we so desperately want to have. Your inner safety is built on micro threads of navigating the doubt, the unworthiness, the misalignment (the self-criticism) and the betrayal - those ways that we want to run from our own ideas either because they sounds absolutely crazy or we undercut our inspiration with self-judgment.

Some of the craziest ideas were my best ones - ranging from unraveling health conditions within my kids, business ideas, even moving houses and yep - restoring my own health and completely transforming myself from within.

When my son (now twenty) was younger, he was ultra-sensitive. From sounds (he hated the vacuum cleaner) to material (he hated jeans), I had to carefully plan outings and wardrobes so that we could mitigate one of his meltdowns. On one rainy day at a soccer game, he flipped out. The rain that was beginning to fall softly on his face freaked him out. And he screamed so badly you'd think the rain was setting him on fire. I wanted to crawl into a hole and die. For real. It was the first time that I knew that something wasn't aligned, I just hadn't known what to do about it. My in-laws were there and later on my husband got a call asking if we had considered that he might be autistic. She thought that for several reasons. As well as his sensitivity, he also walked on his toes. Also, he did not really interact with them. If you added those three features together, that was a typical autism diagnosis. Looking back, I can see why she thought that. Together, it made sense. What I knew though, was that my gut doesn't lie. And my gut said that there was something to figure out; however, a diagnosis of autism was not it.

There is this feeling that I get in my gut when something is just not right. I had this feeling that what he had separate problems going on. And yes, I had tons of people tell me that I was in denial and that I was grieving. I was told that it was time for me to face the truth - get him on meds and give him the best life that I could.

That gut feeling though, the feeling that they were wrong about this, persisted. And I began on a pathway to figure it out. I did start out on the logical pathways - consulting doctors and hearing them out. What I found though, was that most of them did not want to answer my questions. I was even told by one doctor to not "grow a brain."

Here is what I learned from that experience - expert is an ego term. And when I blindly trust experts, I hand over my own innate wisdom and connection. After a few of those experiences, I set up a better system so that I could practice more discernment. I would then consult only those that hold a bank of knowledge and then I would filter it through my own intuition and wisdom. It is in this space that a real yes or no was birthed, ideas bloomed, curiosity flourished and I simply followed it.

I then underwent the process of understanding WHY he was so sensitive - he is highly energetic and had been picking up outside energy from other people and his surroundings. In other words, he is psychic and empathic, which had been overwhelming him on a daily basis.

Because of having so many back-to-back ear infections without tubes ever being put in, the nerves that processed sound (and fine/gross motor skills) were not firing properly- How he was processing stimulus was obstructed. Everything he heard sounded like it had a ring to it. If I had that happen to me, I would be screaming too. After going through all of the pathways (and hoops) to get him assessed, we decided to invest in "The Listening Program" and within three weeks, his sensitivity and inability to focus notably diminished. Sounds like vacuum cleaners and sirens no longer sent him into a tizzy.

I had taken him to see a physical therapist for his tiptoe walking only to be advised to see a paediatric orthopaedic. Then we understood that he was born with a congenital birth defect that shortened his Achilles tendons in both of his legs. He went through surgery to correct his gait and the tiptoe walking ceased.

Three separate events when looked at together painted a very different diagnosis than what he was truly experiencing. By pulling the thread and treating each one individually, I learned a lot and within a year he was a completely different kid - simply more engaged and less agitated. I often think about what it took for me to navigate that pathway because everyone around me thought that I was nuts. What I was free from, though, was the shame and self-judgment.

I was able to separate my vision from their thoughts, opinions and judgments. It was easy for me to do so even though some close to me told me that I was being reckless by not only listening to doctors. I mean, they WERE the experts, weren't they? In this case (and many others), no.

I found that it was easy to go on this pathway for someone else. I easily fought for them on their behalf because they mattered. I brought him here into this world and I was going to protect him at all costs.

What I found exceptionally difficult was beginning this process for myself. Yet when I did, I was able to draw on the feeling, the courage, the curiosity and the strength that I had in those moments and then slide them over into my own journey.

When it came down to it though, building something new mattered because at the end of the pathway was a vision that looked really, really interesting. It was laced with,

 I wonder _____

and then feeling that outcome as if it has already happened.

It's the space between your current reality and this new one that you feel so strongly that you simply take the steps to close the gap between the two spaces.

How we navigate and build unshakable confidence is built on our feelings. The key to accessing your unshakable self-confidence resides in not resisting the shadow pillars. It resides in not believing the shadow pillars. It's "Yes, I'm feeling this AND I have a greater vision." One of the things I started doing in my life is to start planning for the shadow pillars to show up, because they're going to show up; why wouldn't they? They are fantastic way-showers of growth - it is in feeling these spaces and not believing them that we build MORE inner safety and resilience from within.

When I can feel my own feelings, no matter "good" or "bad", no other person's intense emotions can sway me from my center. That is power, rooted in the connection to the wisdom of your highest Self.

First though, you have to feel safe within yourself and in your nervous system in order to allow this to happen. I was giving this some thought today because for the longest time I required my outside relationships to feel safe in order for me to move forward. I wanted their unwavering support on MY journey. The biggest hurdle that I experienced was that I didn't know how to navigate not having it.

This is one of the hurdles that most of my clients experience as well. They want their husband's unwavering support, they want their parents to champion whatever path they're taking, they want their friends to be able to relate to this new version that they want to become. Basically, they are waiting for other people to give them permission to do so because they don't have that safety established from within. They also think that they should feel good while embarking on the journey and if they do not feel good, then something is surely going wrong.

Nothing is going wrong and you are exactly where you are meant to be.

Safety is a feeling that can be cultivated and is 100% necessary on your own personal journey. Most of the time, we end up focusing on how we feel unsafe instead of finding evidence for our safety. In meditation today I was feeling a little uneasy about the steps I am taking to move forward in my own personal development, because our growth is constantly unfolding and expanding. I envisioned my little girl around age five feeling all of the feelings that I'm feeling right now. The difference between her and me is that back then she really was alone, her parents were trying to figure out their own lives, they did not look out for her as well as she needed them to, and she had to figure out a lot of survival mechanisms in order to simply Be Safe.

As I move forward now, those feelings of the past pick up again telling me that I'm not safe because I'm "alone" on this part of the path. When I allow myself to love her exactly as she is and soothe those feelings from within, I take the time to find evidence for how I am supported - within and around, from physical beings to the Unseen forces in the realm. I have to find evidence of my safety on purpose so that I can continue moving forward and take disciplined action. When I don't, I shut down.

I want you to think about the times that you have been supported by others. How did that make you feel? That feeling right there is the one you want to focus on breathing into yourself everyday, multiple times a day. It's not about feeling good BEFORE you take action, it's taking the time to cultivate that safety AND take action - no matter what - towards your vision.

Your family will support you as YOU believe in yourself. That was the biggest revelation that I had throughout my many journeys to follow my visions. I had cultivated an unwavering belief and faith in myself, so much so that my family couldn't help but begin to get on board. As I continued various pathways, from helping to restore my son's health to going about restoring my own, I had unwavering belief in the outcome.

So many people want support before they begin and the only reason they want this is because they lack the emotional safety from within to begin the process from a place of curiosity and faith.

Our inner safety is built on micro threads of navigating the doubt, the unworthiness, the misalignment - right, the self-criticism, the betrayal (when we have an idea and we abort it, because, gosh, it's never going to work). When you move THROUGH these pillars, you deepen your inner safety.

I tend to think of things in triads, and how we move in our life and the combination of our energies. We all have a masculine, feminine and child energy, and it creates a triangle - a triad. When our masculine, feminine, child energy is in alignment, we experience an idea that is lifted up through divine desire and then taken action upon. You know that you are in alignment with yourself fully when it happens (and usually fast): you get this creative inspiration (the divine child) and then an intuitive download (the divine feminine) and then simply take courageous action (the divine masculine). It's like an arrow that has been drawn back and shot straight in. That's being in alignment.

So how do you know, when you're stepping into the shadow pillars, that you're reacting to them and resisting them?

The diagram below shows how the triad responds to fake confidence. When that's going on the masculine shifts from being that really clear, courageous driver of the vision, into an overachiever and performer. The feminine energy moves from this fantastic, nourishing, intuitive connectedness into being an overgiver, like a caregiver on crack. The inner child becomes the good girl into the people pleaser.

When you step into THIS triad (and we all do), it is simply telling you that you are moving towards somebody else's vision or expectation instead of being in your own divine alignment.

(masculine)
The Achiever
becomes the
Performer

(feminine)
The CareTaker
becomes the
Over-Giver

(inner child)
The Good Girl
becomes the People
Pleaser

When you start to understand which shadow pillars are actually ping ponging, then you can start to ask yourself some better questions. Most people are taken by surprise by the shadow pillars. The reason why we get stuck in this energy is because we have past memories attached to them. These memories contain survival strategies that worked for us in the past (hiding, shrinking, pleasing), yet on the pathway of self-discovery and reclaiming our Magic, these do not help us thrive. If you plan for the shadow pillars, you will not be surprised when they show up.

And that is where I want to be - in thriving. It is where I envision my clients being. It's where I envision you being.

That is the reason why mindset plus energy healing is so vital, because what you want to do is really move into the energy centers of the body where those buried memories are held deep within the nervous system and release the hold that they have over your survival brain.

It's not about getting rid of those survival strategies. It's not about fixing them. It's about understanding them powerfully and bringing them to the light of your own divinity. Those wounds turn into wisdom and that wisdom adds to your inner strength, which amplifies your inner safety.

I WAS scared of the side eyes and the deep sighs. It's just that I was scared of death and dying at that time in my life more. So I kept on moving. And as much as my family WAS scared of me leaving the pack mind, they were also more scared of my ill health.

Along the way of my own journey though, something really interesting began happening. They started seeing that I was becoming more connected in myself, I was becoming more vibrant in my life. I was becoming more of me. And it was unveiling something in them that they hadn't seen or felt within before that either. You get to be the leader in your life and then you end up creating a movement within the circle that you are in.

I did not think to create a movement first, it just sort of happened. It began with understanding and allowing myself to plan for these shadow pillars and then glean the wisdom from them. It is how you build unshakable confidence. I'm not telling you that you're going to approach life with a lion's roar. nor should you. Because there are times that you're going to navigate things that feel really fucking scary. And it's okay. And it's normal. And you can navigate it.

In the smallest of ways.

Some of the biggest errors that I experienced and that I see in my clients is they want to make these big leaps in fake confidence, instead of really honoring these small 1% shifts in being willing to navigate the shadow pillars and grow in greater faith, safety and resilience.

I think that it is the 1% shifts that give us the inner safety to practice for the bigger shift. That way you are not faking anything and you will make it to your vision because you have decided to journey towards your own healing.

Do you notice when you make a small shift? I never used to give myself credit for the smaller moments when I felt doubt and navigated it well, moving myself to greater certainty as a result. It was so easy to pass over. Every time I passed over celebrating and acknowledging those small moments, I ensured that I would feel more scared for the bigger moments.

I call it stacking. Stack those moments in your mind, on paper, put it somewhere in front of you because it is those moments that are the evidence of you knowing how to "do" it. They are gentle reminders that if you had the courage in one area that felt a little hard, then you really can have that courage anywhere.

Give it a go - audit this past week. When did you feel doubt or unworthiness or that critical inner voice and STILL persisted in a way that helped you believe in yourself more? Write yourself a letter to yourself and then read it aloud.

Give yourself credit. It's the best way to build self-support and shift into greater confidence.

It's these small micro threaded events celebrated in our life that help us build up the inner safety for the larger events. Truth be told, I got tired of getting sick month after month. And I had this vision that nobody can ever take away from me. It was one of those visions that, to this day, I can still see so clearly. It is the driving force behind why I continue to do this work and how my business was born.

It's okay that you might feel trepidation as you move towards something new. It's normal. Plan for the first layer of feelings, soothe yourself in a healthy way and keep going.

When I'm feeling doubt I actually give myself a timer. I tell myself, "You know what? You can sit in this for the next twenty minutes and then we're going to start shifting out of the energy so that we can start asking ourselves better questions. And yes, I do refer to myself as we, because there are so many parts of myself, right? There's not only my chakra system, but there's the triad of energy: the divine masculine, the divine feminine and the divine child. I talk to myself as a unit; it's kind of funny and entertaining, but it makes me feel like I'm part of a team.

Here is the #1 question that helps me shift out of the pillars - how is this helping me grow?

This is where you let go of the need to feel good and go in faith to GROW.

✧ Go Beyond the White Picket Fence ✧

Download the free workbook and access the tapping video "Accept all of your awesomeness"

https://gromen.lpages.co/beyond-the-white-picket-fence-workbook/

In the next chapter...

I am an only child and both of my parents worked. I was an 80s latch key kid and made a vow to myself that my kids would not experience the same thing.

Aloneness.

When I was a kid, my parents came home and were totally spent. By 7:30pm, my father was on the couch with a tumbler of whiskey in hand and my mom was upstairs tending to the household portion of her responsibilities. By 9pm, she was in bed getting ready to do it again the next day.

There was not a lot of emotional support or encouragement in my home and the way that I got noticed was by doing "good".

Being helpful. Making their life easier, because if it wasn't usually an explosion would happen. Followed by a healthy dose of shame and disappointment because *didn't I know how hard they worked?*

Doing for others to mitigate negative emotions became a habit.

And a people pleaser was born.

Being conditioned from such a young age to shy away from those feelings of shame and disappointment led me to always be there for other people.

For a long time, it made me feel good. I liked being needed and wanted. I liked the praise that I got from others. I liked being "good".

At some point though, everyone began needing me and wanting me. And since saying no was not a skill that I had built, I began to drown in tending to their needs and ignoring my own, so much so that I began to resent it and then shame myself for doing so.

For a long time, I fought it - that little voice that said that I had no more to give. I just silenced that voice with workouts to ease the stress, coffee for the shot of energy that I needed and wine for the come down of the day.

Because saying no felt like the earth was shattering. I felt like I was being mean and selfish for WANTING to say no. And still, I kept on going - saying yes to everything I thought I needed to in order to be a good mom, a good wife and have it all together.

Yet, I had NOTHING together.

My family got the scraps of energy that I had at the end of the day, which were usually snippy and impatient. I was on the couch by 9pm with a glass of wine in my hand.

Grumbling about nobody caring and feeling totally unappreciated in all areas of my life.

Still though, for the longest time, I did not see it. I had recreated my childhood - I WAS my parents and that scared the crap out of me.

And finally, when I grew tired of this daily process, I had been presented with a choice - to stay the same, live in the overloaded expectations that I had been raised with or begin to simplify my life by admitting what I wanted and move towards creating that.

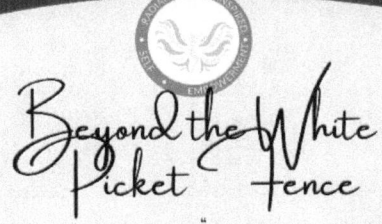

"Healing helps you evict behavior that is no longer working in your life.
From yourself & others."

YOUR OWN LITTLE DEVIL

A small girl stood in front of her mirror and cried because in that moment, she felt so angry and so alone. She did not know that she held the keys to unlock her strength, her wisdom and more love for herself. That little girl was brave. The adult that she would grow into would become the parent that she wished for. That adult would heal and evict the old behaviors that created that feeling of aloneness in the past. She would be stronger than ever; she would be a model for others. Her wounds, when healed, would become her wisdom.

My husband and I started watching the show *Lucifer*.

It's an entertaining show about the devil who comes to Los Angeles, opens a night club and becomes this sort of antihero. He's super-hot.

In the show, there's an angel that always comes back to the nightclub trying to talk Lucifer into coming back to hell and he calls Lucifer 'Lucy' for short. I nearly spit my wine out in laughter because my husband calls me Lucy when the worst parts of me come out.

Omg, I'm like the devil.

Only sometimes, I must add - when Lucy takes the wheel. Proof right here. We all have a little Lucy in us, that part of ourself that is a total shit when she gets hurt. She lashes out like a motherfucker in retaliation. And then possibly has some sort of shame or guilt spiral after the dust settles.

Here's why getting to know Lucy is so damned important. It's this part of us that creates so much shit talk, so much crap in relationships and so much chaos in the world.

It's this part that keeps us in fear.

"What if someone finds out that I am really this broken?

"What if I really am not good?"

"I should be better."

"I know better than to act this way."

This part of us could be called a total asshole and I totally get it. But what if she is NOT?

What if instead of calling Lucy an asshole, I learn to understand her? I learn not to let her control my life or to take the wheel? To discover instead of blame? To reveal instead of shoving her back into the shadows?

To love and understand her because that is what she really needs in order to feel safe in the world instead of wanting to spew darkness. Big life transformations and massive relationship shifts happen when I become aware of when Lucy wants to strike (and why) and then CHOOSE not to use her as part of my communication strategy.

I strike gold in my relationships with awareness every single time. It took me a long time to get to know Lucy for all that she is and all that she carries. It took me a long time to take responsibility for Lucy's behavior instead of looking to those around me to take care of her.

It's not like I am a saint and decided that this part of me needed love and healing and grace. I had an epiphany in the form of, "there has GOT to be another way." Frankly, I got tired of what I felt like in my relationships. Exhausted, Overwhelmed, Stretched, Unappreciated, Resentful and just plain fed up.

Lucy tells me that the problem is ... them. 100% all of the time. And for the longest time, I really did believe it. So, I tried everything to try and change them. I'd offer suggestions for how they could improve. I have this mug that says, "If everyone would listen to me then this world would be perfect."

It IS my Lucy to a tee.

This part of me wants to control everyone's behavior and it happens for a couple of reasons:

If I am controlling them, then I don't have to control myself or my own emotions. I will proudly tell everyone that I know what is best and I will get them to believe me or argue with them until they submit in some way. It's also easy to not make decisions in my own life because I am so focused on them instead.

If I let them control me via this need to people please and make them happy, then I won't have to learn how to build resilience through experiencing emotional discomfort nor will I make decisions for my own well-being and encourage them to make decisions for themselves for their own well-being. I will always take things personally, which will keep my relationships codependent and in constant chaos.

That desire to control only happens because of this super deep fear that I (or they) won't be able to handle the emotional pain and discomfort that comes along with either me setting boundaries with other people or the reaction that I will experience when someone else sets boundaries with me. It keeps us from making clear decisions in our life and then persisting, pivoting or conceding along the pathway to creating our desired result.

When you let Lucy stay behind the driver's wheel, she WILL keep you in the drama triangle - with others and with yourself.

When you are in the drama triangle - you are just ping ponging emotional pain between the inner victim and the inner villain within you. You will know that you are in the drama triangle because you will be rooted in blame.

You will chew on anger. It will definitely be someone else's fault. You will find that your mind goes to how you were fucked over. And any hero story that comes from this space is created from either suppressing your own emotion or oppressing someone else's.

In order to create a really heroic outcome AND a win-win solution for everyone involved, you must stop believing the narrative that is initially being created and be willing to go beyond it.

It's work.

It is not comfortable to move beyond that initial summary, which is:

> Person X does _____ to me and now I feel bad - it must be their fault because I am a nice person. Here is a list of all of the things that I did good and here is a list of all of the things that they did bad.

Viewing people and circumstances from only this perspective is so limiting.

This ensures that we never get to the part where WE take care of our own emotion instead of relying on any outside person or circumstance to do it for us.

It creates division within ourselves, other people and it keeps us from elevating into wisdom, acceptance, discernment and growth.

The drama triangle is rooted firmly in expectation and judgment.

And that causes our internal suffering.

Many people that are stuck in the drama triangle are 100% addicted to their own chaos, their own inner toxicity.

If you crave getting out of chaos, the only way to truly do so is through inner work.

The outside world and those in it are uncontrollable. They have their own life experiences that shape their perspectives and so do you. You cannot change the lens through which they perceive you, the situation and themselves.

However, you can change your lens by healing your relationship with yourself, since all of your interactions are merely a reflection of your own patterns. A deep desire to get out of the chaos is the breadcrumb that leads you on the pathway. The victim perspective is just the first layer of thoughts and feelings to move through.

The villain energy is the second layer.

There are other layers that you will move through as you continue to read this book; those layers will introduce you to other parts of yourself.

By doing so, you learn to take 100% responsibility for the result that has been created in your adult life. And this is an important distinction because what happened in our childhood is not our fault. The people in our lives did not give us what we needed in order to thrive emotionally. As adults, we get to choose to heal the patterns by getting to know how they are showing up in our life today so that we can choose not to react in that fashion anymore.

Your childhood patterns do not have to continue to create chaos in your adult life.

When you choose a different lens of perception through inner healing, you get to think new thoughts and feelings, which creates a totally different set of actions and life movements.

And that creates a new result in your life.

It will connect you to the parts of your mind that are resolved to unite from within instead of divide.

To grow instead of thrashing in stagnation. To stop looking to the outside world and those in it to change in order for you to have more life satisfaction and fulfillment. You will begin to create it yourself, no matter what. Your interactions will become containers to learn more about yourself.

By doing the inner work, you begin to learn how to soothe your Lucy and heal her versus depending on someone else's behavior to dictate her happiness.

You stop slinging negative emotions back and forth, getting underneath those layers to ascertain greater understanding.

When you do, you change your approach by looking at the situation through a lens that is not filled with emotional pain.

I began figuring out who I was by understanding what I did not want

That is how I began to get out of the backwards energy wheel, where I never took care of myself. I had a giant list of *"Do Not Want"* in my life, which meant that I actually DID know what I wanted. I was just scared to say it out loud. I was afraid to be met with resistance.

I was afraid to be bolder in my life by not giving a shit about what other people thought. And really meaning it.

How do you not give a shit about the random person in the store or on social media? Well, it is easy. Meeting resistance from your family or other people that you respect? That can be tough. The feelings of vulnerability can be mistaken for weakness from within and we think that something is going wrong. That moving forward is maybe the wrong choice.

Maybe. It's where your head and your heart are not aligned.

It can make you want to hide or grasp for someone else to just agree with you so that it doesn't feel so scary. Or so alone. It's easy to get someone else's opinion on your path. What you will find is that you end up spending time trying to make them happy.

To align to their reality. Even if it really doesn't fit for you. All the while, your energy is draining little by little and then all at once. And before you know it, your back is against the wall - you find that your overall health is being compromised and you are faced with a choice...

You can choose to step into growth - to create the reality that you want to live in. Or choose "sameness". The funny part is this - you will grow no matter what. I always say, "Struggle on purpose now by choice or be forced to in a much more chaotic way later." This is why I am such a fan of inner work.

I choose to struggle now by intentionally working on healing layers of old thoughts and feelings that are no longer helping me move forward in my life. Suspending your reality by kicking it down the curb only ensures that all of the stuff that you need to heal will accumulate along the way.

That is what feeling stuck really is - an accumulation of energy that needs to be moved in order for your growth, coupled with your unwillingness to move it intentionally. I've been there... #healthcrash. I have also healed on purpose for the past eleven years.

When you heal though, you begin to understand that the resistance in others that you were so afraid to meet and navigate were simply reflections of your own inner critic. Your own fear. Your own judgment.

And that you were never really afraid of their opinions. You were afraid of revealing your own, the ones that have been buried in the dark underneath everyone's expectations. You no longer crave looking kind or good. You begin to create a life centered on holistic joy versus moment to moment immature emotional "management".

In other words, you stop keeping everyone happy.

It is one of the most futile activities that you will do. It will erode your soul and tear apart your life and relationships if you don't get out of the pattern.

Before you can begin to say no, you have to do three things:

Step and root into your conviction.

Build commitment to yourself.

Up your own personal success standards.

Weave your inner healing throughout steps 1-3.

Your conviction in yourself and your vision will guide your forward movement

You are reading this book because you want to create something different in your life. And you have tried so hard to change the behavior of other people to no avail. You are tired and you are weary and you understand that the only person that can create your new reality is you.

The problem is this: when you continue to look outside of you for permission or support, you will continually go back to the pack mind. And it's only when you root into your own conviction that you will allow your vision to expand and your forward movement to go with curiosity.

Your conviction resides within your own internal safety. It resides within healing your nervous system and reminding yourself of how you and everybody else wins when you step into greater levels of personal autonomy.

Conviction will never be cultivated outside of yourself. There is no person around you that can give it to you.

It. Is. Created.

It is created from within. I believe there are three main ingredients for creating conviction.

Your intention. Your actions. Your willingness to make mistakes and learn from them - over and over again.

I used to hate failing and making mistakes. Really hated it. It made me feel stupid and I did not like that feeling. And for the longest time it kept me from feeling more purposeful in my life. It hid behind things like embodying the idea of perfectionism and the need to be a control freak.

I DO like things to work, I love efficiency and I am a leader. To step into that I had to create and cultivate conviction in myself and in my vision. I had to believe that my wanting to create and feel more fulfilled in my life and business was a good thing. I had to believe that I mattered. I had to develop the conviction in that belief - the kind of conviction that allows you to begin setting old behavior aside because it simply no longer fits into who you are becoming.

And I had to be willing to fall down, learn, grow and get back up again. Over and over again. This pathway of growth is an exercise in emotional sovereignty, where you understand and become aware of your own little devil patterns and heal them along with no longer tolerating other people's little devil patterns.

You might openly admit that you no longer want to do laundry at 11 p.m. at night even though you've spent years and years of your life doing so. It's having the understanding deep within your bones that you matter, that your time matters and that up until this point you have trained everybody to drag you and drain you to satisfy feelings of unworthiness from within.

No more.

You must feel that seed of desire for wanting a new way to live and be. And that seed of desire will allow your intention to flourish. Your intention will guide your action. At first, your actions might be to push others to change their behavior in order to accommodate your vision.

Been there and done that. It's only when you begin to have the desire to change YOUR behavior that you create sustainable transformation in your life.

What does having conviction mean for you?

How do you get better mentally, emotionally, spiritually and physically when you decide powerfully that what you are doing in your life is no longer working for you or for them?

Your transformation does not reside in leaving anything in your outside life. It resides in the conviction that you have within yourself and deciding powerfully that you want to create something better in your life. And in being willing to feel the suck while you are doing it.

That requires that you create space from within. That requires that you be willing to navigate feelings that don't feel good and remain convinced of your greater vision. Be willing for nobody to be on board with your plan. And be brave moving forward regardless.

For four minutes a day, I want you to envision your desired feeling. What is the feeling that you will have within yourself when you create what you want?

When I was in the process of restoring my health, I envisioned myself as healthy, whole and feeling good. I envisioned myself in calm interactions. It didn't matter if I experienced emotions that didn't feel good along the way. Sure, there will be times when it feels like you're taking ten steps forward and then twenty steps back. That is the process for growth and when you remember and are rooted in the conviction of what you are looking to create, you will most certainly do so.

What you want to create resides in what you are willing to feel and still believe unwaveringly in the possibility that you can create it … no matter what.

I'm willing to feel anything and experience anything in order to create the results that I'm looking to create. No matter what. I will not quit. I will not run away.

I will, though, pay attention to what is coming up for me so that I can pivot when needed. This requires that you heal your thoughts and feelings. The ones that produce doubt. The ones that drag you into the pits of unworthiness. The ones that criticize you and tell you how awful you are.

You can believe them or you can look them in the eyes, heal them, understand why they are here and stop believing them.

Build commitment to yourself

When I began this work, it was so easy for me to break promises to myself. And I convinced myself that me not taking care of myself was giving more energy to them. Now, I did not actively think about how I was not taking care of myself. I actively thought about being of service to THEM; taking care of them, not wanting them to be mad or unhappy with me. I did not want them to think that I did not care.

And when the bough broke for me, I had to decide something different - to care about me and focus my energy in a new way that honored myself and them. Some people did not like it and that was part of the process of building commitment to myself.

Before stepping into greater self-commitment, taking care of myself and my needs, I told myself that it was selfish for me to be thinking of myself. I will tell you a secret, though. I wasn't serving from this place of joy and energetic reserves. I was empty and really frustrated because I wondered why people didn't care about me. I was giving my all 150% of the time and I was running on fumes.

I resented them and myself. The mistake that I made is that I thought I was hiding it. Nope. I was giving them my pain and I didn't even know it. I thought that I was just being a nice person. What I did not realize was that my "good girl" was on call and working hard.

It was that part of me that sacrificed myself for everyone, just wanting them to be happy. I was selling my soul off for praise and adoration - either from my family seeking happiness or from clients seeking security, money, adoration, etc.

The freedom that I created when I plugged up the leaks, drains and stopped sacrificing myself was everything. And what I created within my body, home and relationships was a new template for communication and self-care.

We are all hard wired for service. Period. So it becomes the personal inner work to consistently shift from being in self-sacrifice to serving from a place of joy - and that can only come from your own decision to build commitment to taking care of yourself and your own needs so that you are full from within instead of looking for outside sources to fuel you and fill you up.

I was saying this in a talk today at a networking group. I used to go to bed feeling bone tired - the kind of tired where I wondered if any of it mattered. Then I healed and moved to the space of building more commitment to myself. I then went to bed tired yet fulfilled. It was in this space that I realized my need for doing was still dragging on my energy and dragging on the way that I showed up within my relationships.

I decided to learn an entirely new form of sustainability so that when I go to bed, I still feel like I have energy. I have given joyfully to them and to myself so that my energy has been constant.

Once you commit to connecting to your own Universal energy and love, the game changes and you will feel more alive than ever.

This commitment to yourself can begin showing up in the smallest of ways. The other day, I put on a sports bra from Victoria's Secret and the underwire was sticking out into my rib cage. I would grumble to myself about how uncomfortable this bra was, yet I did not take the time to throw it out.

I told myself that when I took it off that night I would immediately throw it into the trash. You guessed it, I never threw that bra into the trash. The next week I went to put that bra on again and I stopped myself in my tracks and reminded myself that I hated this bra. It made me uncomfortable and left me with cuts on my side. I then remembered that I had made a promise to myself to throw it away and I laughed at myself about how easy it was to let go of that commitment to take care of myself in all ways.

The old thought of, "I don't have time," reared its ugly head. Why didn't I take the time to just throw the bra away and select a comfier one to wear right then and there?

What does a sports bra have to do with anything? How we do one thing is how we do everything. It gave me a beautiful reminder to re-examine myself and my relationship with myself, and myself and my relationship with others to see where I have been telling myself that I don't have time and I have been allowing myself to suffer as a result.

How has, "I don't have time," kept me from experiencing the fullness of who I am?

How has, "I don't have time," kept me in anxiety and disconnection?

How has, "I don't have time," shown me that I am not taking care of my needs?

How has, "I don't have time," strained my relationship with myself and others?

I'm not asking you to inventory how you break promises to yourself as a shame exercise. Shame only binds you to pain and keeps you from moving forward. Answering these questions allows you to decide powerfully what you'd like to experience more of and then create the space for that to happen.

YOU matter. Your energy matters. What you want to experience matters and the only person that can create it is you. You are the governor of your time - not the other way around.

∼

Up your own personal success standards

∼

I think most people are living by an old manual. They don't even realize it. Where you were five years ago and the operating thoughts and feelings that you created from is not where you need to be now. It will take the desire for a new way of living and the willingness to go through an experience before shadow pillars along the way for you to up your own personal success standards.

Just because you have allowed clients to contact you at 10 p.m. in the past does not mean that you need to experience that anymore. You have to be willing to update your own terms and conditions. That means setting new standards and being willing to become your own best supporter even when it feels like ass on a stick.

The mini transformations that you make on a daily basis happen through your decisions. It is stepping into your own self integrity and honesty to determine what decisions you need to make. Every decision that you make helps you elevate your own personal living standards. You are no longer living your life according to the expectations of your parents, your spouse, your kids, or the fucking PTA - you are courageously being honest with yourself so that you can build a new level of trust with yourself, heighten your intuition and live in your truth.

This elevation of your personal standard happens in a simple four-step process that I call DUHS.

Like, DUHS - it's so simple anyone can do it.

It's simple, not easy. When you begin to implement this process over and over and over again you create this willingness and momentum to create massive transformation in your life on all levels. It becomes easy because you are building this foundation on personal conviction and commitment to yourself because your growth and transformation brings forth a new model for everyone.

DUHS stands for:

> **D**ecide
> **U**nderstand that you will feel uncomfortable emotions
> **H**ave your own back no matter what
> **S**oothe yourself (because that is how you get through the emotional discomfort)

Most people don't go through the process of consistent transformation because of the emotional discomfort that they experience. Let's face it, we are not taught as kids how to navigate emotional discomfort. Our parents had no idea what the fuck they were doing when it came to navigating their emotions, so they basically shamed us or bullied us into stopping, whether it was crying or laughing or being too loud or too expressive or too creative.

This process gives you an actual pathway to follow that allows you to acknowledge the fact that you're going to experience emotional discomfort as you transform your life. The actions and the steps are so simple; it is the navigation of the old thoughts and feelings that we have buried within our survival mode-based brain and body.

We have trauma buried. Even if you had a fantastic childhood, you are more than likely left with some sort of thought that you need to behave a certain way in order to get people to like you. And that is worth healing so that you can live in a greater level of full expression, honesty and vulnerability with yourself. It is how you connect to you - the unique Divine wisdom that is pertinent for your journey here on this Earth.

As you go through the healing process and you get to know yourself better, you step into this part of you at a greater and greater and greater level.

My four-step process for elevating your personal standards

1. DECIDE.

Decide powerfully whatever it is you want to transform - from throwing away an old bra to repainting a room to no longer taking a phone call from a friend that drains your energy or deciding a specific time limit for which you will talk to that friend or family member. Decide powerfully no matter what, understanding why this decision is the best for you, your time, your energy, and how you show up in all parts of your life (family and business). And don't betray yourself by flip-flopping and changing your mind, especially when this decision is you taking the best care of yourself.

Many times we talk ourselves out of our decisions because of the little shitty voice that tells us we are a mean bitch for wanting to elevate our own personal standards. When we decide to no longer tolerate something that we know is not working in our lives, we become more powerful, but there is a little shitty voice inside of all of us that will undercut that decision as fast as you make it.

When you understand how you fuck yourself with a shitty narrative then you can become aware of it, heal it and not believe it, allowing you to move forward powerfully.

So decide, even when that little shitty voice rises up and tells you that you're a total asshole for wanting to implement this new standard into your life.

2. UNDERSTAND THAT YOU ARE GOING TO HAVE UNCOMFORTABLE EMOTIONS.

The asshole voice should come as no surprise to you. We all have one. If you understand that you have a default scenario that wants to be loved, that wants to be liked, that wants to be good and impact the world - and you know that part of you has been hijacked by other people's opinions of what that looks like, then you will know that you will be met with a critical voice every single time you decide powerfully to elevate your own standards.

Anytime you elevate your own standards, you are going to intentionally ignite the shitty voice so that you can learn how to heal it. Many times we believe the shitty voice, we turn our backs on our decision and we end up betraying ourselves. We don't even realize that we're doing it because it is so fucking easy to do. It sounds so normal, so believable and what we do step-by-step is turn our back on ourselves and give our power away to somebody else's opinion or expectation of what makes a good person, a good woman, a good wife, a good mom, a good businessperson. Understand that when you make a decision to elevate your own personal success standards, that shitty voice is going to automatically start firing. It is not about believing, it is about healing it so that you can continue to take action forward towards moving into living your best life as your best self in your own personal success standards.

When you live by your own personal success standards, you live in greater levels of joy. And when you live in greater levels of joy so are those around you and that is service.

To understand that you are going to have uncomfortable emotions and intentionally move forward anyway is the pathway of the Sovereign being. You can access the wholeness and the freedom within you, being truthful with who you are and how you want to be in this world so that you can also be the model for other people around you to do and be the same.

3. HAVE YOUR OWN BACK.

You begin to have your own back when you allow yourself to have the shitty voice, expect it to be there and not believe it. When you make a decision, you have clear reasons for doing so. You have clear evidence for why this decision will benefit you, your life, your family, and your business. It is this part that you need to remind yourself of when the asshole voice starts kicking in.

When another person has an opinion or a reaction from your decision, the asshole voice will automatically kick in, saying, "I'm so mean", "They hate me!", "Maybe I am super selfish", "I can't do it", "I am not a good mom, wife or person", "I'm a hot mess," or my favorite, "I suck." Those are all normal default thoughts of the survival brain. This is the part of us that just wants to be part of the tribe no matter what, no matter how much we have to bend over backwards and compromise ourselves, no matter how much we have to deplete ourselves and stress ourselves out, no matter how much we give of ourselves. There's a part of us that will happily shelve our own decisions and desires for other people's praise and adulation.

It's normal.

Yet, you don't have to believe that voice. When it kicks in, you can have your own back by reminding yourself of the benefits of taking a new pathway in your life. You can remind yourself of the powerful new transformations and results created by your new thought process. When you think and feel healthier beliefs and you take action in that mindset, you create new results in your life. When you learn how to take care of yourself powerfully, you create more in your life. You are more honest with yourself and that will bring massive amounts of clarity, discernment and wisdom.

Every time you believe the asshole voice and you listen to it, you betray yourself. Having your own back is understanding that the voice is going to show up and it's going to rattle the cages of all of your old patterns hoping that you turn back and go back to the old ways of your life, yet not believing a word of it so that you can continue moving forward.

This is the space where you learn to enjoy the ride and embrace the suck.

Make no mistake, it sucks to feel shitty. You know what sucks more? Lying to yourself and to all of your relationships. Not loving your life even in the struggles. Wondering what went wrong and how you have spent so much time feeling empty and sad about your life. Regret is the worst.

Having your own back means that you are 100% honest with yourself, willing to honor the decisions that you make and be willing to feel all of the feelings and have all of the thoughts while continuing on the pathway to your transformation.

4. SOOTHE YOURSELF.

Soothing yourself is simply nurturing yourself while maintaining the discipline levels required in order to move forward. It's so easy to tell ourselves, "Buck the fuck up and keep going!" and yet that's not what we need in order to move forward.

I've discovered that a healthy dose of discipline, self-nurture and fun are the necessary components of walking through the halls of change with the asshole voice in tow. Soothing yourself requires that you accept that asshole voice. We all have parts of us that are scared to move forward. We all have modeling from our parents that keeps us from being more honest and vulnerable with ourselves. We all have those parts and the more that you treat them with some TLC, the easier the pathway is to navigate.

Soothing yourself doesn't mean believing the asshole voice. it means that you are going to be gentle and loving towards that part of you that is fearful, yet you are going to move forward. It's taking fear, judgment, shame and giving it a seat at the table to voice its concerns without allowing it to have decision-making power.

How you react in the drama triangle is powerful. When these behaviors kick up, you can understand yourself and show up to soothe yourself with more grace and understanding and that leads to greater levels of acceptance and reduced levels of resistance.

It is the resistance that keeps us stuck - not the actual emotions themselves.

I recently made a series of decisions that honored my own bandwidth, in my coaching business and in the shared business that I have with my husband. I decided to ask for help, outsource and build business with what feels like leveled energy instead of burnout rocket fuel.

In the eyes of others, it is a slowdown. Admitting all of these changes out loud to other women who are actively building and scaling their own businesses felt hard. This is because most women have tied their empowerment to their ability to create their own wealth. To retire their husbands. To impact large numbers of people in the world.

I usually witness them living in overwhelm, exhaustion and burnout without allowing themselves to honor their bandwidth. They typically end up sacrificing their most sacred relationships as part of the process. That is not what I want. It's not my dream to be a girl boss with an imbalanced home life.

Admitting that and then making the necessary changes to support that in a sea of peers doing the opposite takes a centeredness from within that has been years in the making.

My dream is to continue to be an active presence in my teens' lives, and to grow my partnership with my husband - I have always said that if you want to really explore partnership with your spouse, go into business together.

It's fun though, even when we hit a snag. We have two separate roles which, when they come together, are magic.

It's also my dream to grow my own coaching business filled with clients who cannot wait to do the inner work.

I continue to simplify. To ask myself how I am showing up within my priorities - myself, my family, my business. Do I feel like I am getting As and Bs? What might be creating drag? I get a choice, change my thoughts and feelings about them so that I can experience more calm and joy or I will choose to change the circumstance altogether.

Simplify. You will soar in all areas of your life when you are not focusing your energy on everything. Simplify to soar.

To move forward though - you DO have to go backwards. You need to become aware of and understand the parts of you that have kept you from making yourself a priority in your own life.

Then you can heal them and welcome all parts of yourself home.

Go Beyond the White Picket Fence

Download my Free workbook and access 9 steps to unapologetic confidence.

https://gromen.lpages.co/beyond-the-white-picket-fence-workbook/

In the next chapter...

You will change as you heal.

It's admitting to others that you have that brings a lot of stress and uneasiness until you decide powerfully that it doesn't have to feel that way for you.

About a year after I began deeper energy healing, I no longer enjoyed being at large in person events, concerts, markets and so on. In those places, I felt like I was in an energy vice.

It took me going to a few shows and really feeling energy-pummeled to begin not only admitting to myself that things needed to change but admitting it to others too.

At first it felt weird to say, "I'll only be sitting here for about an hour then I'm going to go outside for a bit." When I did though, I felt more true to myself. More honest and more whole. And more in control of my energy and myself.

I simply tweaked and adjusted to a process that worked for me instead of ignoring the needs of my healed self. Some people acted weird and those people just don't hang out with me anymore. And that's okay. Others think nothing of it and that's okay too.

It was my decision to be okay with myself that has compelled me to show up more powerfully and truthfully in my life. As I accept myself fully, those that care for me deeply do so too.

A few weeks ago, Luke bought me tickets to see Kings of Leon at an outdoor venue. He said, "I got lawn seats since I know the pavilion makes you feel weird."

True love. Partnership. Acceptance. And let's not forget fun.

It began within first. I no longer experienced the energy vice and you don't have to either. Inner truth grows your light within and your strength. If you're struggling with your healing, your growth and you feel that energy vice, let's talk. Amplify your energy instead of being pummeled by it.

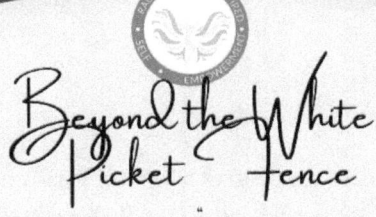

"You are NOT broken and don't need fixing - you have been living according to someone else's expectations and guidelines for life. You can begin to do the inner work that leaves the baggage in the past and takes the lessons and gifts with you."

HEALING YOUR LUCY

Once upon a time there was a young girl who felt like she was unlovable no matter how hard she tried to get that love. For most of her life, she thought that love was from others. As she healed, she learned that it is created from within. She never looked for love outside of herself again. Love from other people was simply icing on the cake.

Self-awareness is the key to healing your Lucy and transforming your life. It's where your childhood patterns no longer create the results in your adult life.

You are made up of three parts:

Your Divinity - that part of you that is connected to God, The Universe, All That Is. Some call this the "Higher Self" or "The Soul". I will use both terms when I speak about this part of us.

Your upbringing (Your Lucy) - the survival-based patterns that you have learned in this lifetime (and so many others). It's this part that is the immature ego and needs healing. It keeps you firmly seated in the drama triangle when you do not.

Your healing - where you take the time to heal the wounds of your upbringing and turn them into wisdom. This is where your matured and healed Lucy begins working with your Higher Self to create more inspired goodness in your life.

It's in this balanced triad that you will have greater inspired thoughts and feelings, which will lead to greater inspired actions in your life.

When Lucy takes over and you get in a rut, you will be able to slow down, connect to your Higher Self, and tend to the part of you that requires healing (either through self-work or working with someone else to help facilitate the healing).

Getting to know yourself better through the five love languages.

Because I was spending so much of my time pleasing other people, I never got to know myself. In the midst of my immune system crash, I was forced to make a choice – and that choice led me on a journey of self-awareness.

Up until that point, I felt alone. I felt lost. And even though I was surrounded by people who loved me, I still could not fully feel that loving feeling within. I was convinced that something was wrong or broken within me. Before the crash, I simply did more because I thought that I would find the lock and key to my happiness outside of myself. Little did I know that the path of looking outside of ourself for happiness is a fool's errand. And yet, here I was seeking everything outside of myself. No matter what amount of enjoyment I experienced, I just could not fully feel it.

It was like there was this veneer over my heart that was not allowing that outside happiness to permeate my inside. And it left me feeling not good enough. There were always these whispers – in the darkest times of my life, within my darkest thoughts that maybe I was not good enough, maybe I was not lovable, maybe I really did not matter.

I was certain that I was a massive disappointment in my life.

And then I would have these countering thoughts. Thoughts that said, "You do matter; you have gifts that will be shared with the world. Keep going." Those thoughts would keep me sustained through those dark times when my self-judgment took hold.

The fact of the matter is, I had no idea what I needed in order to feel loved or emotionally nourished. Up until my journey began eleven years ago, I was still fully living for everyone else's expectations – their wants, their needs, their desires, their way.

I was dependent upon their praise for my emotional nourishment. I enjoyed the quick hit and then searched for the next one. I felt needy, always searching for ways to get that feeling and make it last.

Then I came across a book that changed my life *The Five Love Languages* by Gary Chapman[1]. This book explained that we, as individuals, fall into five categories and that these categories will point us in a direction that determines how we want and need to be loved.

This book was essential in transforming my relationships because that information alone was so profound. When I began showing my loved ones appreciation in their own love language, they felt emotionally nourished. What I did not want, though, was to continue to depend on them to speak to me in my own language.

Through deeper reflection, I realized that this book wasn't giving me the answers for my own self-love until I turned the lessons from the book inward. That was the ticket I had been really looking for and it was a fabulous way to begin to love and honor myself on a whole new level.

If you do not know your own language – you are being loved in someone else's love language, and when that happens you will not feel loved fully because their love language is not yours. The intentions to love are there; however, we are not in a space to fully receive that person's love.

It's kind of like reading a book in a foreign language. There is a message there, however, the ease in decoding and acknowledging their message poses a challenge.

The five Love Languages are:

Words of Affirmation
Acts of Service
Physical Touch
Quality Time
Gifts

I got to understand why I love quality time so much and why I find ways to spend time with myself that FEEL nourishing and recharging for me. I got to buy myself clothes, sheets, towels and blankets that simply felt good - soft, stretchy, while still matching my style.

It gave me a gateway to fall in love with myself in a new way. And that elevated my Self-esteem and Trust in me.

As I became aware of what my own personal love language was, I could not only begin creating personal experiences that would give me the self-love and emotional nourishment that I had been craving, I could ALSO begin letting those I love know what my love language was so that they could show their love in a way that would hit my heart and fill up my tank without depending on them to fill it up. When you give love to yourself, anything outside feels like the icing on the cake.

This became incredibly profound because everyone around me has a totally different love language. I am a quality time and physical touch person. My husband and oldest son are words of affirmations people. My middle son is an acts of service person. My youngest son is a gifts and quality time person.

What does this mean? That each of them interprets and absorbs loving energy in a different way. And unless you know what your love language is AND you also know the love language of your loved ones, you will lead from your own love language. And what about those who know nothing about love languages at all? They simply repeat what they have been raised with even if they have hated that way, because it's what they know. Think about this: what happens when you do not feel seen, heard or valued? You do not feel connected and that is what we really crave within our lives.

My mother's love language is gifts. My father's love language was words of affirmations. Mine was quality time and physical touch. My mother bought me a ton of gifts - still does. My father would tell me what a good job I was doing followed by a, "You could do better." Truth be told, my father always struggled with crippling self-criticism and felt like he was never enough, so to strictly give a compliment and then let it go? It wasn't going to happen because he would not do that for himself. They thought that they were making me feel loved by what they were doing. And I knew that they loved me. What happened from here was a lot of miscommunication because I felt completely unloved - and here is the reason why:

My parents did not really hug me or spend time with me. And the ways that they did never landed because I was pushed past my energetic limits (crowds drain me), which led to them getting angry (why aren't you grateful?), me getting punished and then getting an apology followed by a hug. I learned to associate my love language with pain, which just kept me from actually letting it in.

As a person who has re-parented herself, I get it. They were both single parents trying to figure out how to live their lives, feel love themselves and they wanted me to fit into a box, not give them a hard time and keep them happy. They did not know how to "deal" with a child that they deemed sensitive. Of course, I craved connection and since none of us knew about the power of love languages, I spent my time getting into trouble as a younger girl and teen because some attention was better than no attention. I spent a lot of time with my grandmother, who understood what I needed. Looking back, I am betting that quality time was her love language, so we just jived.

However, when it came to receiving that from my parents, they did not know themselves or me. When they went to give love to me, they expressed their love language instead of expressing it from mine. And because of that, their expressions of love never hit the mark; it's like the love tank was being aimed for yet the love was splashing all over the sides versus ending up inside the tank.

What did that lack of love look like in my life? I chased around relationships as a teen. I desperately wanted to feel loved and cherished. I was super needy. I tried to mimic what others thought was sexy. I wanted to find someone that would spend time with me. Because I did not have the greatest modeling for how healthy relationships worked, I ended up surrounding myself with people who were also struggling to feel loved. From the ages of 12-16, I got involved in substance abuse early and engaged in unhealthy and abusive relationships before meeting my husband.

I carried the energy of desperation and because of that desperate need to feel loved, I aligned with people who were emotionally unavailable. I did not know any better, all I knew was that somebody was finally paying attention to me, even if it was in ways that made me hustle for attention or felt like I was less than.

The perceptions that I created within my childhood sounded something like this: "I must not be lovable." "I must be bad" "I am not good enough." Was I told this? No, not at all - however, since my parents did not speak to me in my love language, I did not fully feel loved and valued.

Coupled with my upbringing and experiences in general, I even grew to hate receiving gifts because I felt like I was being bought off out of guilt from my parents being divorced. I have since discovered that I was not being bought off. My mother's love languages was gifts so she was trying to emotionally nourish me by using her love language.

My father spoke words of affirmation (his love language), yet that is not my love language. What ended up being created within me was a superwoman that chased achievements and praise from others.

I used to blame my parents for my emotional pain, which kept me from healing them for a really long period of time. It wasn't until I got tired of feeling so isolated and empty that I chose to begin my own inner work. My childhood wasn't my fault, my healing (as an adult) is my responsibility. It has made me a better parent to myself, a better parent to my kids and a better partner in my relationship.

Parenting comes with no manual. It does, though, come with a bag full of old patterns and those patterns are perpetuated because we do not know any better. I had a talk with my mom because that understanding that she wasn't just buying me off was huge. She really was trying to love me. Now, when I receive gifts from her, I know that it's her way of saying *I love you*. I also let her know what my love language is - so she now makes an effort to invite me to go places and do things with her, honoring my love language.

I also know that when I buy her a gift or flowers, she feels immensely loved.

All that I can say is that it's powerful to have a simple piece of information, apply that information into your own life and watch everything in your life and relationships explode into technicolor.

This can happen all because you decide to become aware and begin to take care of nourishing yourself in ways that align to you.

This basic breakdown of your love language will allow you to deepen your relationship with yourself as well as deepen and strengthen your relationship with your loved ones when you learn to express love to them in their love language and you encourage them to express it to you in yours.

You can find out what your love language is here: www/5lovelanguages.com/profile.

Once you pinpoint your own love language, begin living it unapologetically. Speak kindly to yourself in the mirror daily. Take care of yourself. Buy yourself something that will make you smile and feel connected inside. Spend time with yourself - take a walk or watch a film or read a favorite book. Massage yourself with your favorite lotion or wrap yourself in the softest and most delicious blanket.

When you begin really loving yourself with your own love language, you will feel more connected to yourself. You will be more honest with yourself. You can even ask your loved ones to take a quick and easy test that will help them ascertain their love language or you can go on a fun quest to figure out what their language is.

What did I find when I finally began living and loving in my own language and loving other people in theirs? Connection, communication and a vibration of love that hummed throughout the house and throughout my life. Amazing things happen when you begin to love people in their own love language; they begin to feel loved and they look to see what your love language is. If they do not know, tell them. It's okay to give them that kind of direction. We are talking about feeling loved and feeling connection in your life, so do not make your loved ones guess how to love you when now you know!

Why does my oldest son spend time with me? Because he feels loved when I affirm his awesomeness to him, he looks to give love in a way that I receive it best. I believe that it's how we humans have been designed, to feel connection - we crave it. The one piece that we are missing though is filling up our own tank properly. Because the main connection that we are meant to have is with ourselves.

As we do, we fill our tank up (and keep it filled) so that we can lend our energy to those people and experiences that keep the well flowing. We then extend connection outward, building a ripple effect of clear connection and communication.

I sat down with them to let them know of my revelation because they will have spouses and children that have different love languages and they are going to want to know how to speak to them so that their tank gets filled rather than splashing all over the surface.

What does loving yourself even begin to look like? I WAS going to the salon and getting massages, but I did not feel any better. I did not feel filled up. In all honesty, it felt like another to-do. Sure, I liked the way that I looked or felt at that moment, but the moment was fleeting. And then when something happened that triggered me, I went into a tailspin.

And that is because although I was doing self-care, I was not practicing self-love. And it continued to leave me feeling unlovable - that old childhood wound would keep creeping in.

Because although we are not unlovable, at times we can sure feel like it. As you determine your own love language, begin to give love in that way to yourself. For me, it meant alone time that felt inspired. Inspired alone time was any time that I spent by myself doing something that I loved. It also included doing nothing at all. I believe that as women we do not do enough of that. It was time unapologetically carved out for myself and my own needs and desires without needing to tend to anyone else.

We have relied on outside sources to love us and that is a problem for a couple of reasons. Most people are emotionally unavailable, meaning that they have not had a role model of someone that has shown them unconditional love in their lives. Also, most people do not even know their own love language, let alone yours. Yes, we are in the midst of a lot of closed off people. In the past, that caused a lot of pain because we have been errantly relying on them to love us. However, when we learn to honor our love language first, we fill ourselves up and then we begin to live from a space of openness as a beacon of light within the darkness.

We are caregivers and nurturers because it's in our nature and because we have been trained to be that way. We have not, however, been conditioned to take breaks and fill up our tanks in the way that we need them to be filled. Once you get in the habit (five days and beyond, because that is how long it takes to build that habitual muscle) of loving yourself, then you can share your love language with everyone and ask them to love you in your language.

No matter what, though, give it to yourself.

By going down the rabbit hole of self-awareness, we take ownership of our energy which means that *we are responsible* for our feelings, our thoughts and our belief systems as well as taking the time to unwind misperceptions that have been created because we have been relying on others to fill up our cup.

When we get to know ourself better, we begin to realize that we are normal. And we are also enough. Up until this point, you might have been under the impression that there has been something wrong with you.

You are NOT broken and don't need fixing - you have been living according to someone else's expectations and guidelines for life. You have been trying to get love and validation from others using their love language rather than understanding that you speak a love language all your own.

⭐ Go Beyond the White Picket Fence ⭐

What is your love language?

Download the Free workbook here.
https://gromen.lpages.co/beyond-the-white-picket-fence-workbook/

In the next chapter...

When you're not honest with yourself, you will not support yourself. And when you don't support yourself, you can't have your own back. If you don't have your own back then other people's opinions will sway you, making you think and feel awful things about yourself when they are not happy with you.

I used to think that showing up to everything is what made me a good mom. I stretched and drove (oh, so many miles in a giant square) and really exhausted myself. I usually ended up missing something key because I was trying to be everything to everyone. This caused me to chastise myself incessantly. Because of how awful this felt, I simply ran harder to please others. What I found was that happiness is fleeting and because I didn't have my own back, once the happiness ran out, I felt deep unworthiness.

These best intentions just volleyed exhaustion and resentment between us. They were unhappy and I was unhappy. It turned out my need to be all the things was creating lots of disconnect in my life - within and around.

It occurred to me at a time when I was at my breaking point that there had to be another way. One decision I made to finally support myself and be honest with myself changed the game.

You know why being everything to everyone did not make me a good mom? Because I wasn't present. Because I was irritable when I got back home. Because I ended up feeling like I was wasting time and felt really disorganized. Because I expected them to be the same way as me - do for me as I did for them, which was completely unhealthy. And no one around me really appreciated it anyway. Or if they did, it was fleeting.

The truth was, I didn't appreciate me. I was not honest with myself or them out of fear of disappointment from them and then feeling all of the yuck that goes with that.

It wasn't until I got 100% honest with myself that I began the process of healing those inner stories that said, 'I'm not enough unless I'm doing for others.'

I decided that I am enough. And that decision led me on a journey that has created loads of internal freedom.

I can decide to feel enough now too. Healing creates your internal freedom.

- Be more present.
- Be more joyful by the end of the day.
- Be more organized.

You give others what you give yourself from a place of honest, unconditional love.

Sometimes that means saying no. Sometimes that means choosing one thing over another. Sometimes that means others will be disappointed. And still - you are safe and okay.

As you heal, you become more honest with yourself. You support yourself. You lean into your wisdom. It's in this place that outside opinions don't impact or sway you.

"The only toxic relationship that I ever had was the one that I had with myself. Everyone else was just a reflection of that."

~Author Unknown

TAKING LUCY OUT OF THE DRIVER'S SEAT AND RE-DISCOVER YOUR POWER

Once upon a time, a young girl looked out of the window from a high tower wishing that others could see her in the way that she wanted to be seen. What she did not realize was that they saw her as she saw herself. And when she began to see herself in the same way that she wanted others to see her, she unlearned what was keeping her locked away from knowing herself and loving herself more. This gave her the courage to come out of the tower and be seen as who she really was.

Your soul has always known the pathway; it's been waiting patiently for your Lucy to get on board.

Most of my clients come to me because they are experiencing uncontrollable anxiety. It has been consuming them for a long time, they have autoimmune disorders and they are always tired.

A lot of the time, they are frustrated with their family or co-workers, convinced that if they would just change their behavior then the household would run smoother. And because of old patterns, they just do more of whatever to try to make others happy. This makes them feel empty, disconnected and anxious in their lives.

That is the first way that the wounds of your inner child (or your Lucy) begin to appear.

As kids we are told to push through or shut down any emotion. How many times did my parents tell me that if I kept on crying, they would give me something to cry about?

I learned fast to shut down my emotions for my safety. As an adult, it shows up as people pleasing, needing to know, trying to avoid making mistakes and then all of the shit talk if something goes awry.

Anxiety is your inner child sounding the fire alarms that something feels unsafe to them. Most of the time, before doing this work, we push through it. And here is why that ends up screwing you:

You ignore your own Lucy instead of soothing her.

You leak life force energy when your nervous system goes hyperactive.

You miss the opportunity to take care of yourself, root in your own self-knowing and build resilience.

That pushing through it? It's your inner adult that is telling your inner child, "We don't have time for this shit, buck up."

I used to do this too.

How many times did I know that I needed to say no but did not have the inner safety created to say no and navigate all of the emotions within that I would experience? How many times did I remain small because of the old energy that told me that I was unsafe? Anxiety can come at us from both sides and it's the awareness that is created that allows us to move forward having our own back or pull back (set a boundary) and STILL have our own back.

This cocktail of mismanaged intense emotions creates anxiety. Not knowing.

~

Anxiety is buried under fake confidence. It's how you maintain control.

~

For real, every person that I work with struggles with control.

If they are more Type B, they struggle with controlling what others think of them - they want to be viewed as kind, good ... unselfish. They will run themselves into the ground doing for others and if they even think that they have made someone else mad, they experience anxiety through worry.

If they are Type A, they struggle with controlling what others think of them - they want to be viewed as self-assured, confident ... secure.

My Type A-ers run themselves into the ground by proving their worth through achieving. Achieving makes them feel like they are on top of the world. If they fail, they experience anxiety through worry, self-doubt and massive judgment.

It may show up in different flavors, which is why it's so important to learn about how your Lucy shows up in life - in the good times and in the times that feel bad.

Anxiety is where expectations and the need to control them intersect. It is where you live in the past and pull that pattern forward and it automatically creates the future while robbing you of the present moment. It is where we use each other to find peace instead of turning inward to find out what the hell is going on and begin to set new standards to live by.

When you DO know, then you can prepare for how you want to respond rather than letting Lucy take control and then simply react.

Reacting does two things:

It makes someone else responsible for your emotions. No wonder you are feeling so out of control and anxious. Right? It's us giving away our power for someone else to manage it.

It keeps you from mastering the skill of re-parenting yourself, giving yourself the approval and acceptance that you need. Up until this point you have been searching for it within others.

I have a secret for you. Those people don't know how to accept and approve of themselves; therefore, you will never get it from them. You will just meet their wounds. This is just a reflection of your own. Fascinating, right?

In one of my meditation sessions, I was told this: "The soul knows when the ego is at the point where it is receptive to healing. It is the point where one can no longer ignore their intense emotions or do something to get out of them."

Our soul has this magnificent intelligence. Your Lucy has been aware of its presence but has also decided that she could (and should) be able to figure things out on her own.

The biggest hurdle with this is that our wounded self is trying to heal with knowledge of ONLY wounds.

It's why when we hit our lowest point that we finally surrender to healing and integrating with our divine wisdom. Lucy avoids it for so long because in order to heal, the fears that created the wounds must be faced and healed from a place of love - not from talking it out over and over again.

My clients also experience a lot of overwhelm and exhaustion, which can be directly related to avoiding the anxiety. The constant doing comes from the desire to not feel anxiety. If they are always in motion, then they can ignore or numb out the anxiety. When it gets too great to bear though, you become aware of it and decide that it is time to "fix it".

Most want to just get rid of it without actually addressing inner behaviors and transforming them. That is why anxiety ends up being this recurring "condition" that does not go away.

It CAN though, through awareness and deciding to gain new perspectives on that feeling in your body and what it is trying to convey to you. And if you allow that awareness to lead you on a healing journey, you will discover greater inner freedom than you have ever known.

Anxiety is a feeling in the body. Many times, my clients think that something has gone wrong when they feel anxious. That is not the case, it's simply that they are feeling a feeling that is uncomfortable and they cannot shove it away.

I used to have horrible anxiety and I usually escaped it by being busy. It helped me numb myself out. I also used to work out to get "rid" of the anxiety. I trained my body to get used to the workout high or I was completely numb, so whenever I felt anxious it felt awful and uncontrollable.

When I began perceiving my anxiety as a marker or intel from my body, I could take a deeper look to see what was going on with Lucy so that I could learn to soothe her and powerfully have my own back. Usually it was telling me that I was betraying myself in some way, either in pushing myself when I needed rest or not setting a boundary when I knew that I ought to be.

Or perhaps I had set a boundary and my Lucy was freaking out over perceived backlash. Or I was stepping outside of my comfort zone by making a bold move in my life or business.

Anxiety is normal. It is not a problem when we see it as a marker and then take a look at what it's trying to tell you from within so that you can feel it, have your own back and learn to soothe it while still moving forward.

Recognize and acknowledge it in your body.

Breathe. Two counts in and six counts out. This intentionally activates the parasympathetic nervous system so that you will feel calmer.

What story are you telling yourself? Write it out. Many times, we don't take the time to write out our intense thoughts. When you can see it on paper, you firstly get it out of your body And secondly see the full story that your Lucy (the inner victim and villain) are telling you. You get to read it out loud and let the emotions flow while you tap on your collarbone, heart, stomach, head to free the emotion that is trapped and stuffed away in your body.

Take the time to write it on paper. So many times, there is a fear attached behind the anxiety. The inner child is completely freaked out and the inner adult is shutting it down over and over again.

Healing requires that you not only transform your thoughts, you have to get into the nervous system response and soothe it. Most of the time, people want to bypass that step because they think that vulnerability is weakness. And it's a lie that your Lucy is telling you.

Soothe your nervous system and step into greater clarity.

Then affirm your safety. In this moment, recognize where your needs ARE already met.

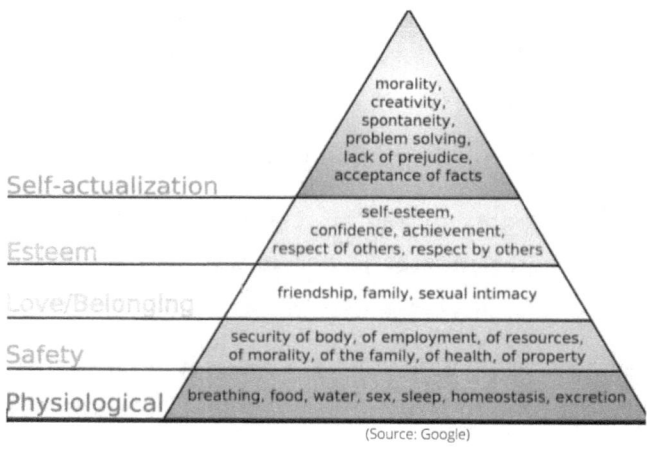

(Source: Google)

I don't know about you, but I cannot tell you how many times my parents tried to shut down any "tantrums" or other intense emotions and without even knowing it I adopted those coping skills into my adult life.

Feel the anxiety on purpose instead of shoving it away like your least favorite smell. What does that feeling feel like in your body? Where is it located? Does it have a color? If it could talk, what would it say? Anxiety is your Lucy trying to keep you from feeling another intense emotion that you are not used to feeling. What is that feeling?

Envision that area within your body being wrapped in a warm and loving embrace. Breathe slowly and allow the feeling to pass without the need to shove it away.

Meet your anxiety with less resistance and more acceptance - the control that it has had over you will begin to diminish. As that feeling neutralizes, you can then ask yourself some different questions that will help you create new perspectives and make new decisions on how to proceed.

Here's where I think people get caught up in taking care of other people's needs over their own. We, as a society, get caught up in wanting to heal the community when we need to be focusing on healing the aspects of ourselves that are rolling around in the drama triangle.

I think that community service is important. However, I believe that a lot of community service is done as a result of Lucy projecting (seeing the wound in someone else and not recognizing that it's a mirror of your own) and spiritual bypassing. I used to do this too. I would see a need in the community and fill it instead of recognizing that that is also a need that I have to heal from within. When I heal it from within, I have a completely different perspective so that when I do serve in the community I am not doing so from a need to save or rescue other people. I am serving from a space of joy, understanding that those who I am serving might not receive it as I intended and how it is received is none of my business.

I believe that Maslow's hierarchy of needs is super important and vital to our own spiritual growth.

Yes, when you are moving forward and making decisions to take care of yourself, your emotional safety is going to feel wobbly. It is important to affirm your own safety and have your own back so that you can move forward.

The healing always looks like this:

You.
Your family, as in, how you are showing up and behaving in your relationships.
Service in your community from a place of joy, presence and clarity, not from saving, rescuing and sacrificing yourself.

Many people think of having their needs fulfilled through material and physical wealth. There is nothing wrong with this. I think that our material and physical wealth are a reflection of our ability to feel safe to receive and be responsible for abundance. If we don't feel abundant though or are trying to hustle for our worth, no amount of material and physical wealth will feel sufficient.

When I am talking about this though, I am looking through the lens of emotional wealth and prosperity. If I am serving from a place of pity or needing to save another person, I am actually serving from emotional poverty and that needs to be healed from within in order to feel more whole and complete in this world.

I was sitting on an airplane recently and I had a conversation with the person sitting next to me. She was a woman in her twenties. I learned that she was in the process of setting up her own business.

That's terrific.

She agreed and then she blew out a big breath. She then told me that the reason why it's happening is not so terrific in her eyes. She said that she had been let go recently from a job, a job with a Fortune 500 company that she loved. This woman began the job at the age of sixteen and climbed the ropes. Her job was a good paying job; she had acquired many skills along the way.

And two months ago she was fired.

Tears began to stream down her face as she began telling me a story about a co-worker that did not like her, the one that had it in for her, the one that she was so nice to, yet she never cracked the hard covered shell of the woman. Her victim energy was taking over the conversation.

I listened as she recounted the number of times that she had done extra work for the woman. She cut her hours for the woman when she had heard that the co-worker needed them instead. There were so many ways that she felt like she was over-extending kindness in the hopes that maybe this co-worker would like her a bit more than the day before. Of course, that did not happen.

Cue the villain energy chiming in. The frustration mounted within this woman, yet not knowing any other way, she kept on doing things for this woman hoping that the co-worker would begin liking her.

As this woman on the plane spoke, her eyes narrowed. "Nothing I ever did was good enough for this woman," she said. She then told me that the final straw and her dismissal happened on a Thursday afternoon when she lost her shit at this co-worker.

Her villain energy said one phrase out loud that sealed her fate: "I just want to destroy this entire place and everyone in it."

An unfortunate thought, fueled by intense anger uncontrolled and it put a final nail in the coffin for her HR report. She was sent home and a few days later received the phone call from her direct superior that she no longer would be employed at this Fortune 500 company.

They told her that, of course, they hated to make that phone call. That she had done such great work and had a lot of growth potential there.

BUT what she said, even in a fit of anger, was a direct violation of policy and required her dismissal. Oh man, that sucks. It really sucks. As she was telling me this story, tears streamed down her face.

She told me how unfair it was. How she was still fuming at the co-worker. And in our conversation, she was extremely certain that it was all this other person's fault, that this co-worker who had been treating her poorly was the cause and the root of her frustration.

She was convinced that she was the victim. She was convinced that the actions the company took were uncalled for, that they were unjustified. Add that to the healthy dose of shame that she was feeling for "fucking it all up" and you have a recipe for the drama triangle.

She was convinced that if this co-worker had just been nicer, it would never have happened. I offered to present another option so that she could learn and grow from this experience, so that she could begin her business in a new energy so that she could get herself out of the drama triangle.

All the situations we have are an opportunity to grow. To better understand ourselves and examine why we do what we do, how we create our own results and what needs to change in order for us to create a new reality.

She was blinding herself to greater awareness by only looking through the lens of emotional pain. She was making herself the victim by only talking about how nice she had been, how helpful she had been, how much of a good and hard worker she was. Until she expanded her awareness and asked new questions, she would repeat this experience over and over again.

It is all true; she is a nice person, a hard worker and super helpful. That was evident by how quickly she had risen within the company, yet there were some glaring red flags that were popping out to my coach mind.

She was not friends with this person; as a matter of fact, she confused being co-workers with friendship.

She expected reciprocity from someone that was unwilling to give it.

She was living in a one-sided relationship.

She was not setting any boundaries.

She had been taking this co-worker's opinion personally and therefore doing more to seek her approval.

She felt guilty for her own success within the company so she was dimming herself down to try to make the other person feel better.

Because she was younger - she was falling into a child/elder role versus owning her gifts, talents and abilities and seeing herself as an equal contributor.

She was making the other person the villain, spending time since being released from the job talking badly about the co-worker to people. She spent time justifying her blow-up and shaming herself in the process. Not even knowing it, she was being the villain to herself AND the other person.

She was simply trying to feel better. To locate and step into the hero of the story. The hero that she was trying to locate will never really be found in the drama triangle. Sure, that might be found for a brief moment in time when she tells herself, "I am better off. Now I can start the dream that I have had. Now I can be my own boss."

For a moment in time, she will feel her independence and freedom, until she thinks about the entire situation again. As that happens, she will bounce back and forth in the drama triangle until SHE decides to get herself out of it.

My question? How is this helping her grow and step forward into the next chapter of her life without the baggage of the past? Being stuck between these emotional reactions will keep the drama alive instead of using the circumstance to dig deeper into her own thoughts and feelings.

When you are in the drama triangle, you will try to make yourself a hero by making the other person wrong. You will make the other person responsible for making you feel better, and how many times has THAT been a recipe for success? Sure, you might find some relief in the short term. However, without awareness and the practice of awareness, it's so easy to slip back into the creature comfort habit of chaos.

You give your power away without even realizing it. Blame, shame, guilt - they all put your power into the hands of your wounds (Lucy), the other person or the circumstance.

This is why this work is SO fucking valuable - you finally get to take control of your emotional state in a healthy way instead of being whiplashed by a situation.

How long will she chew on this termination and the players involved? The answer is, once she gets so tired of being in it and not being able to get out of it. Elizabeth Gilbert says that it is when you are tired of your own bullshit; it's true.

Basically, her Lucy will try to solve it from a place of the drama triangle, which only fetishizes wounds versus getting real clarity around the pattern that created the result.

I feel the need to highlight this because many people get caught up in an interpretation that is misleading and it will keep you from being willing to dig deeper to heal your Lucy.

Taking responsibility for your own emotional state does not mean that everything is your fault. We cannot predict the players or the outcome of events. You can, with practice, learn about

YOU - how you approach your life and take the necessary steps to gain awareness so that you can choose a different way to respond rather than reacting from emotional pain.

Placing fault only triggers anger and shame. Moving THROUGH those feelings to attain awareness and breed more wisdom and discernment from within. Once you understand how to take your power back without needing another person to be part of the process, you really become a hero in your own life. Intense and mismanaged emotions are no longer at the forefront of your decision-making process.

You will spend less time vacillating between taking things personally and feeling guilty about losing your shit than actually moving forward for growth. Inner healing allows you to move beyond making decisions out of emotional pain, which always produce dire consequences and keep you in emotional poverty.

Go Beyond the White Picket Fence

Download the Free Workbook here:
https://gromen.lpages.co/beyond-the-white-picket-fence-workbook/

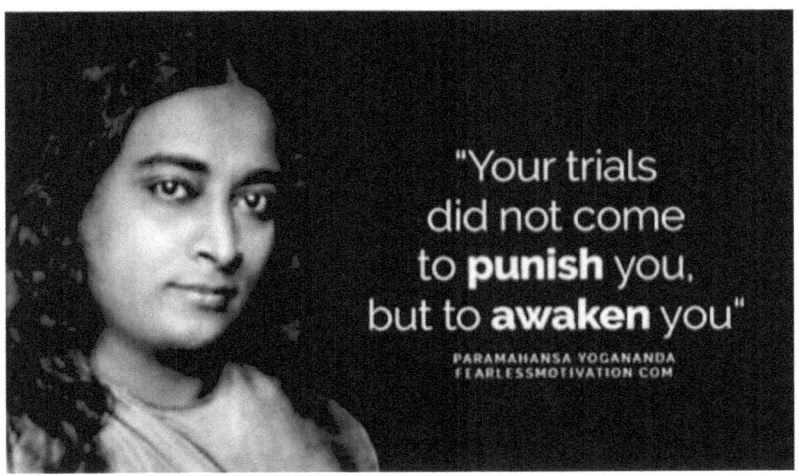

(Source: Google)

In the next chapter...

 "You'll never survive without me; I made you who you are."

This was the parting statement I heard as I turned my back to walk out the door. I had just quit my job. I remember that day so well. Nine years of an identity in my life coming to a close.

I could tell you that this comment alone fueled me to soar and prove to her that I would survive. Yet it didn't. I would spend the next few months vacillating between feeling really sad and in shock.

Did I really just quit my job? Did I really just blow up what I thought was a friendship? Did I really just walk away from nine years of training and teaching for something totally new?

Yes; yes, I did.

The one thing I never regretted? Choosing myself. What I realized was that I did not know how to be my own best friend. I didn't know how to NOT fit in and simply be my own person. Leaving was the day that I gave myself permission to rediscover me.

It took confidence - a subtle kind that was simply there through it all. Through doubt. Through unworthiness. Through all that self-criticism. Through that little voice that said, "You might not survive because you are alone now."

It's all normal and we are led to think it's not. I believe that they are markers LEADING us back home to ourselves. There is this unshakable confidence that we all have inside of us - our Magic. It is just that sometimes we forget about it and believe others and their opinions instead.

MY parting words as I left the room were, "I am no longer living your dreams; it is time to live my own."

I did and have been firmly on that pathway for the past ten years.

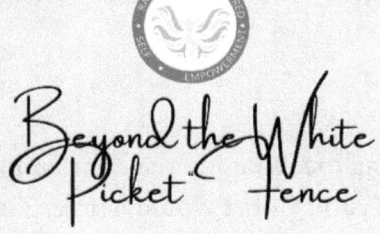

Grow - on purpose. It is where you create internal freedom for yourself.

GAINING PERSPECTIVE IS THE BALM THAT SOOTHES LUCY AND MOVES YOU FORWARD

A young woman looked upon the door and felt the fear of speaking her Truth. "What would happen?" she wondered to herself. Change was afoot and for the first time, she was walking with it hand in hand instead of ignoring that still small voice. Here is what she DID know - that she loved herself… no matter what. It was the first time, yet it would not be the last.

When you decide powerfully to transform your life, you must be ready for your Lucy to fight you hard. Don't be surprised by it.

It feels kind of delicious and comfortable to stay in your default emotional patterns, even when it is chaotic. That chaos is comfort to Lucy. It would be easier to just throw blame, shame and guilt around.

The greater desire of living a calm life is what drives me to dig deeper and ask myself better questions.

When I left my job in 2012, it would have been so easy to talk about my old boss and drag her name through the mud. I thought we were friends - kind of like the lady on the plane did with her co-worker. I gave nine years of my life to where I worked and I really enjoyed it. When it ended, it did so because I made a choice to finally choose myself and my health.

I got talked about behind my back and it felt awful.

In time, I began to not want to roll around in that level of chaos anymore, but that meant that my Lucy had to be willing to grow and that the other part of me (my spirituality) growing would continue to strengthen and gently remind Lucy of our desire for growth.

That becomes the work - growth on purpose.

I came out of the drama triangle on purpose because I grew tired of the middle school shenanigans. MY middle school shenanigans. When I healed the way that I was reacting versus responding, then I got out of the gossip.

I become a better friend to myself and others. I grow in my discernment not only in what I focus my energy on, but with whom. Everytime that I free myself from my own Lucy patterns and desire for drama, I do not step into it with others.

That is freedom.

It was only through this desire to get out of the chaos that I would begin to create and implement the exercise below.

Whenever I am in the drama triangle, I use the five windows exercise to help me feel all of my feelings as well as gain new perspectives on the situation, the other person and myself. Perceiving anything through only one lens ensures that you will be in chaos forever. You won't grow and you will recreate the experience over and over again.

With this exercise and the commitment to self-awareness, you heal your Lucy. You decide powerfully to take full responsibility for yourself and respond versus react. It's empowering.

It's you taking care of you instead of being dependent on anything outside of you to take care of you or make you feel "good enough" in your life. No matter how you are feeling, you are always good enough. You are always worthy. But sometimes Lucy forgets that and when she does, she will want to burn down the world and everyone in it to reassert her worth and relevance.

There are always three parts to all communications: the thoughts and feelings that we have about ourselves, the thoughts and feelings that we have about the other person and the thoughts and feelings that we have about the situation itself.

Imagine that you put the situation in the middle of a room and envision that there are five windows surrounding this situation. Windows of perspective give you intel into your Lucy and beyond, for healing, for greater revelation and to build greater empowerment and safety within yourself.

The "Five windows" process to creating more clarity from within:

Identify the situation:

_____

Window 1 - The Perspective of the Inner Victim and the Inner Villain - getting yourself BEYOND the drama triangle.

When you feel victimized (disempowered in any way), how do you show up?

What do you think? What do you feel? How do you act?

You can think of a current scenario where you felt slighted, offended or horrendously hurt.

Write it out? Get it all on paper and allow that part of you that feels so hurt to speak.

THAT is your inner victim.

For the longest time, I did not know what to do with that part of me that felt totally taken advantage of, disappointed or emotionally hurt.

I would do what any person would - I would emotionally retaliate through the use of my Lucy.

Luke always says that the best defence is a good offence - and I know how to manoeuvre and ready myself for attack. We all do. We don't know what to do with our victim energy, so we store it up and use it for our villain.

Ever get pissed from feeling like you've been taken advantage of and then just allow yourself to "go off"?

That is you harnessing the intense emotions and then hurling them out away from you.

It feels REALLY good in the moment, yet, when all has burned to the ground and the dust settles, that is when the guilt and shame set in.

The victim energy, unmanaged in a healthy way, actually fuels abuse of other people and of yourself.

Guilt. Shame. Blame.

All the blowback of using the victim/villain energy to communicate with people.

And here is the kick in the ass - the reason that this energy combo stays alive is because of the shame that we feel. It's so intense that we just sweep the whole thing under the rug, slightly dying on the inside that we even have this part of us.

It's certainly not holy. However, it is of God. Of course it is, and now you get to begin learning how not to use it in your communications with yourself or others.

"Well, if you didn't act that way, I would not have said XYZ!"

I would justify my behavior and never actually dig into healing it so that I learned how to respond versus react from my emotional wounds.

When you get to know how Lucy shows up when she feels emotionally hurt and then begin to not involve anyone else in making her feel better, you begin to transform. You grow stronger and become more confident. You stop feeling like you don't matter in your life because you are no longer making anyone or anything else responsible for providing that for you. You learn how to create it from within.

And that emotional discomfort? That becomes the fuel that you will use for your growth. On purpose.

First thing first though, you have to learn how to experience the first emotional reaction AND create space from it at the same time.

For me, it began with understanding what Lucy was creating within my relationships. My teens began to distance themselves from me because I was grasping on to them the way that a child might crush a bird. The more they grew, the tighter my grasp became and the more they rebelled.

It hurt and for the longest time, I was convinced that it was them.

I was this great mother, their lifelong supporter and cheerleader and they were leaving me. I felt like Beverly Goldberg. If you haven't watched that show, it's fucking hilarious. Bonus if you grew up in the 80s because it will be endless flashbacks to the stuff that you loved as a kid.

And, if it resonates with your family, you will come to be known as "smother". It's been my nickname for quite some time now, which is even funnier since I have healed my patterns. It's a great reminder that Lucy unbridled is the relationship destroyer.

I have deep compassion for Lucy. She is afraid to be abandoned. Of course she is, my parents got divorced when I was three and then proceeded to make some of the shittiest decisions over the next five years that would result in some of the greatest healing that I have ever known.

Before that though, it was the root of my anxiety. For real.

She is afraid of being left behind. She has trust issues. She is afraid of failing and of looking stupid. She loves the spotlight when she has mastered something. She loathes the process of beginning something new.

Here's how to get to know some of your deepest "Lucy" patterns:

- How do you think and feel when you are afraid of being left out or abandoned?
- How do you think and feel when you fail? What do you do?
- How do you think and feel when you are rejected? What do you do?
- How do you think and feel when you are embarrassed? What do you do?
- How do you think and feel when you are betrayed? What do you do?

You will begin to ask yourself these questions and want to change them when you are fed up. When you realize that your relationships are being destroyed one thought and feeling at a time. Marriages don't just suddenly fail - they fail by one thought/feeling/action at a time. They fail because one person is convinced that it's only the other person that is the problem.

Our kids don't just get married and then distance themselves from us because of their "overbearing wife". There were cracks way before that.

When you get tired of thinking that the other person needs to change, you will begin to look at the only person that truly transforms your relationship. You.

I think of it as true surrender because your Lucy is finally so tired that she is looking to save herself. Your healing is acceptance for all parts of yourself. It is learning to parlay that acceptance into more love for yourself overall over and over again. Your healing creates ripples into your relationships. Your healing IS service. Your Lucy wounds will turn into wisdom and discernment.

I love Lucy so much. She has suffered deep pain and held onto it trying to survive. And because you are ready to learn a new way to navigate your emotions, Lucy will finally get the love that she has been looking for from everyone else.

As you become more aware of how Lucy is showing up in your life and learn how to meet and heal her, you will not depend on others to do it for you.

You will create the inner safety and contentment that you have been searching for from within instead of out there from people that are struggling with their own Lucy.

⚡ Go Beyond the White Picket Fence ⚡

Download the free workbook here:

https://gromen.lpages.co/beyond-the-white-picket-fence-workbook/

More for Window 1 - De-escalating your own anger.

How do you get out of your own victim energy? It's so easy to stay emotionally attached and ensnared to those drama triangle narratives. It's the reason why, up until this point, you have not been inspired to move past them. They are luscious and feel really good to use in the moment. When I am blazing angry, I can feel it rise up my spine. I can taste what it would feel like to say exactly what I think in that moment. I also know the damage that it does to myself and other people, which is why I have strived to learn how to not only control it in the form of biting my tongue, but to learn how to heal it so that the energy that I am biting back doesn't cause blowback in my own body.

The reason I had my health collapse was because of all of the intense emotions that I was choking down and not managing within myself. Sure, I wasn't reacting to other people on a regular basis, yet every day there was a frustration that I choked on, which is why I lost my voice. There are emotions - sadness and guilt - that I continually held on to and never navigated which caused my chronic fatigue syndrome and adrenal fatigue syndrome and fibromyalgia and rheumatoid arthritis to begin surfacing.

It is essential to taking the time to learn how to manage your own intense emotions so that you don't react to other people, as well as learn how to heal it within you so that it doesn't blowback ON you. You need this in order to move forward in this life and create better communication in your relationships and within yourself. How you talk to yourself is how you navigate in your relationships. How your relationships are navigated is, in fact, the way that your internal energy functions too.

It's in Clarity that you are able to have wisdom and discernment. It is where we create our own inner safety and it is that inner safety that cultivates win-win equitable solutions within our relationships.

Window 2 - How is this entire scenario helping me grow?

Every experience is meant for our growth. I'll repeat that: every experience is meant for our growth. There are so many times where we get caught up in the victim and the villain energy and we sit there in it because we don't want to ask ourselves better questions. It is easier in the moment to put it off on somebody else and make it their responsibility that we have got angry or sad or defensive or hurt. When we understand that every experience is meant for our growth, we take the time to acknowledge and embrace it so that we can soothe the victim and villain energy.

It's possible that you were meant to speak your truth and so the particular experience that you're having is allowing you to stand firmly in your power and learn how to have your own back instead of requiring somebody else to do it for you. Maybe you need to learn independence and what it feels like to go out on your own and achieve a goal when it feels like nobody has your back. That will allow you to grow into greater levels of self-trust and resilience.

Growth doesn't always feel good. As a matter of fact, growth can often feel like ass on a stick. It's part of the reason we tend to roll around and volley the victim energy and the villain energy back and forth between people.

By being willing to ask yourself better questions, you intentionally remove yourself from the drama. You no longer require another person to work out your emotions, de-escalate your own intense feelings and gain Clarity. You now have the tools to do it yourself so that when you do go back to communicate with somebody it will be from a place of mature communication. It will be from a place of integrity and honesty and self-worth.

Every experience is meant for your growth and in this window you get a very clear opportunity to find out how it is you're growing. If your brain says that it doesn't know, ask yourself this question:

"If I did know, what would it be?"

Quitting my job was me finally choosing me. I broke a huge lifetime pattern that day - one of always putting myself last. I was willing to put two feet in the dirt and say, "I have a dream and I don't want to do this to myself anymore."

I grew in my own empowerment, for sure. I also realized that I could have spoken up more or communicated differently looking back. I am a much different communicator and leader now and I attribute that to every way that I grew from that experience. Working there allowed me to grow in a way that I would not have otherwise, quitting there propelled me even more. It's in this space that I can look upon my past and understand that it was all for my growth.

I redefined friendship. I understood that a lot of what I did was me looking for praise, adoration and worth outside of myself. I did not know how to be a good friend to myself or how to have a reciprocal friendship. Not having either of those there helped me to grow into the friend that I am today - to myself and to others.

You're always stepping into greater levels of wisdom, calm, love, acceptance - for yourself and other people.

It's in these questions that you become a much more powerful self-advocate and conscious creator. It is where you align with your higher self, your wisdom and understanding how Lucy is navigating in your life without allowing her to continue to do so.

Window 3 - How would my highest wisdom respond and view this scenario?

I like to think of my higher self as being able to view things from an eagle's perspective. There are many times that the drama triangle will put us in the weeds of a scenario. We won't look past what our Lucy wants to see in that moment. This means we tend to roll around in a lot of really intense emotions for a great deal of time before we actually decide to move to Window Three.

I love acknowledging what it is I'm growing into because of the experience I'm going through. That allows me to move into this window where I get to talk to my higher self. Our higher self is that part of us that is connected to God, the Universe, the Creator, all that is. It is our divine knowing. When we look through this lens, our higher self partners with Lucy so that Lucy can feel supported in this world instead of wondering if she is safe and reacting from an old wound.

If you were to put on a set of glasses that allowed you to immediately connect to and see the whole situation through the eyes of wisdom, what would that part of you say? How would she perceive the situation?

It is this part of us that understands that we are all Divine beings with a Lucy in the driver's seat until we decide to take her out of it and heal to mature her.

It was time for me to grow - to have my own dreams and follow them and to acknowledge that back in 2012, I was just different. After my father died, I changed. Nobody else did and that is okay. What my soul needed could no longer be provided in that space. And that is okay.

Through wisdom, I got to really work through the hurt of the drama triangle and see the entire situation through the perspective of a wise magi.

Neither of us is "wrong". And it's okay that I am doing what is right for me and that she was upset. It's okay that I did not understand why she did not understand. I understood myself and even though the path forward was not so clear, it was my path to carve out and that was everything.

When you can look at any scenario through the eyes of wisdom, you will have a more expansive, in-depth perspective around the scenario. You will learn how to have your own back, powerfully show up for yourself and infuse a little more grace into yourself and into the other person in the situation.

Window 4 - How would an objective party view this scenario?

If an objective party was observing the scenario, how would they perceive it? Many times, we try to tell our side of the story to get other people to side with us. I like to think of it as crowd-sourcing information and gathering mob forces behind us. If we asked somebody to have a completely objective opinion though, what would their perception of the situation be?

I want you to imagine a complete stranger across the street witnessing this interaction or situation between you and another person - how would they do it? The reason I love this particular exercise is because it places some neutrality on the event.

It gives you an opportunity to see it from a neutral perspective - one that is not good or bad, it simply is. When you look to de-escalate your intense emotions the goal is to move yourself to greater levels of neutrality. I find that it is easier to move to greater levels of neutrality when I move through the windows exercise.

I think of all of us sitting at a table - my higher self, the neutral party, my victim, my villain, my intention to heal - I want to give them all a voice so that it can all get worked out of my own body. If I choose not to navigate it, I more than likely will swallow down my intense emotions. It's why we have blowups and why we have massive health conditions. What we are not willing to heal from within will show up as declined physical health.

Biting your tongue is simply the first step - if you don't know how to move and process the intense emotions that you feel, you will damage your mind, body and spirit without ever knowing it or meaning to.

I think of myself leaving my job back in 2012 and an objective party saying, "Endings are normal." Period. End of story. No hurt feelings, no drama - endings are normal - they lead to new beginnings.

Window 5 - How can I lean into understanding, acceptance and compassion?

The goal of the five Windows exercise is to understand that perspectives are subjective, so both parties will automatically think that they are right. The victim in the villain will never want to acknowledge that another person's perspective is right. They will always want you to be right and the other person to be wrong. I think they will always want to oppress another person in order to come out on top.

And that is where we always have chaos in relationships. It's where codependency is rooted and stays. Going through these windows is really you allowing yourself to gain greater levels of perspective so that you can not only have your own back and soothe yourself when you are feeling badly - you can learn how to step into your own wisdom on purpose and begin to look at the situation from the eyes of the other person as well.

You may or you may not change your mind, but with greater levels of perspective from greater, more expansive, more loving energy you can have more grace and compassion for yourself and the other person.

Going through the five Windows exercise allows you to move from intense negative emotion to greater levels of neutrality, acceptance and reassurance. It puts you in the position to forgive yourself for allowing your Lucy to drive the car in your life.

Most people struggle with the concept of forgiveness. They think that it is a release of responsibility. They think that they are in some way taking blame for something that happens to them. None of what you went through is your fault. As a child, none of what you went through or experienced was your fault. All of our decision-making beliefs are solidified at the age of ten. The reason this work becomes so important is because we get an opportunity to see how our ten-year-old self has been the decision-making driver in our life through the drama triangle. Forgiveness allows you to become aware of this part of self and take the necessary steps to forgive, understand, heal and release the hold the wound has had over your decision-making process up until now.

Through the five windows exercise, I can completely see why my boss was so mad when I left. I can see that she felt horrifically abandoned and possibly like my quitting came out of left field. I understand how she felt taken advantage of since she had trained me all of those years. She did not change, I did and she did not know what happened. Not being able to understand caused her to lash out in anger and hurt.

You begin to find the wounds within you and heal them on purpose so that you can heal the divide from within and learn how to powerfully communicate with mature wisdom instead of the wounds.

I was able to forgive myself for not communicating better with myself. I was able to forgive myself for abandoning myself all of those years before. I was able to see that my boss was a powerful mirror for me; she showed me how I had been victimizing and abusing myself.

Deciding to quit was not really a reflection on her, it was a reflection on my own growth from within. It was an acknowledgement that some old wounds from my childhood had been making the decisions in my life as an adult. As I re-discovered compassion for myself and forgiveness for the part of me that constantly overworked for somebody else's praise, I could then forgive her for her behavior.

That did not change my mind. It was time for me to fly and there is not one day that I regret that choice. Understanding her perspective though, allowed me to let go of the hurt that I had. And when that hurt from within was soothed, the anger that I felt burned less and less. To this day, I send her universal love and good wishes for everything that I became as a result of knowing her. She has no idea, but she was one of my greatest teachers.

When you begin to harness the wisdom from the wound - you become a powerful creator of your experience. You no longer get ensnared in the mind drama of people and events because you have a way to move through your thoughts and feelings in a healthy way. You learn to powerfully speak your truth instead of speaking from a place with a drama triangle.

Moving through the five Windows exercise allows you to amplify your self-awareness. It allows you to show up for and soothe the emotional discomfort that you are feeling. It helps you to have greater understanding and compassion for yourself, the other person and the situation.

You come out of this exercise stronger and more confident in yourself. You tap into the wisest parts of yourself.

It will give you the inner resolve that you need to either stand powerfully in a boundary that you have set or give you the clarity and wisdom to set that boundary knowing that it is what is best for everyone involved.

It will give you the opportunity to celebrate another person setting a boundary with you.

You will deepen your knowledge and implementation of the foundations of communication - honor, respect, and appreciation for yourself and for the other person. It is where you can powerfully disagree with somebody else without making them a horrible person in your mind.

And because of this exercise, you will have a ton of brain space for creativity to pursue your own path instead of the mental load of the drama triangle.

In the next chapter...

The people around you treat you better when you decide to treat yourself better.

It's ALL patterns. That is it. What you tolerate resides in your own energy field. What you give out, you receive.

The good news? That can be healed. And when it is healed - you show up differently to your own life.

You make decisions (the ones that you thought you'd never have the strength to make) more often because you know that being true to yourself makes everyone better.

You stop behaving in ways that keep you and others small. You grow. On purpose.

Decide. Today.

To grow instead of giving and receiving loads of emotional shit.

The greatest kindness that you can give in your world is you doing your inner work every day.

∼

⭒ **Go Beyond the White Picket Fence** ⭒

Download the Free Workbook here:

https://gromen.lpages.co/beyond-the-white-picket-fence-workbook/

∼

The moment that you gather the courage to LEARN how to say no and stick with it - you rebuild your life from the inside out.

HEART COJONES

Once upon a time there was a young girl that was told that she was "bad" for saying no. And because of it, her Magic faded away and was replaced by deeds. And all through her life, she tried and tried to make others happy until she had nothing left to give. She discovered that her Magic came back every time she was true to herself and said no when it simply did not feel right.

In order to create a life that feels fulfilled, satisfied and centered, you have to be willing to toss happiness out the door.

When you only focus on happiness, you will bind yourself emotionally to another person's desires, give yourself away in ways that you hadn't even imagined and grow resentful of your life, of your relationships and of your business.

You'll also expect others to do it for you.

You'll then give yourself a healthy dose of shame and guilt for wanting your life to feel different. This only stifles the feelings of discontent and gives them a place to grow in frustration.

It's this unwillingness to toss happiness aside that keeps you volleying emotional goo back and forth.

No thank you.

We have all been at that space above. It's when you're ready to leave there (and mean it) that your freedom begins.

Hallelujah!

When you toss happiness out the door, you opt for growth instead. You believe that no one needs to be saved or rescued. You rediscover why your needs matter and you commit to taking care of them unapologetically because everyone wins when you do. You understand that you ARE a good person even when another person doesn't think so.

You are here for growth and every single interaction is an opportunity:

- To be more honest and transparent with yourself and others.
- To model new behavior in your life that allows you to thrive.
- To feel the guilt, shame and other ick and celebrate you meeting your growth edge and surpassing it.

Who you are is not who you used to be. Ask yourself this - have you updated your own manual? Because to grow, you need some new parameters that take care of you instead of depleting you.

That happens one decision at a time. When you answer that question and embark on the journey to create that new parameter, you'll feel more connected to yourself and more satisfied in your life.

Your love language and living by it creates more inner safety within you. You begin to notice what you have been chasing after. You begin to understand that you have been making decisions that actually compromise yourself and feed your wounds. When you feel safer from within, you will begin to identify your own core values and live from them without apologizing. When you do, you will create a life from your own vision and identity instead of looking outside to "try on" the identities of others (and then wondering why you don't feel fulfilled).

It's in this space that you can begin to look at your life a little bit more objectively. You can decide, on purpose, to take the gifts from your past and leave the baggage behind. You admit what's working in your life and what needs changing. You make yourself a priority and go beyond that to build a new foundation from within. You begin to understand that saying no is kindness and love for all of you.

And this, this is really important, you will no longer require your family to be the ones who change. You will stop making them responsible for your feelings. You will stop telling yourself stories that keep you and them small.

You will stop waiting for other people to get on board with the changes you want to make in your life. You will develop a strong backbone from within to stand up for yourself and speak your Truth, no matter who feels inconvenienced or irritated along the way.

You give yourself permission to elevate your own success standards and think of yourself in a new way, which allows you to say no with guilt.

My husband tells me that I have big cojones, and this is true because that ability to have big cojones only means that I have an extremely loving heart and clear self-expression. I have clarity and transparency in who I am and what I want to experience in this life. There is this inherent conviction and commitment to taking care of my own needs, focusing my energy only where I want it to be and moving in my life with such intentionality that I am walking in the best version of myself - for me, my family, and then moving outward into the world.

Basically, I don't want to feel like an exhausted, overwhelmed, resentful, drained bitch. And through the inner work and my commitment to living MY Truth, that no longer happens.

And for the longest time I was making everyone else in my life responsible for that.

I began understanding that I was living my life by three very important principles as I stepped into doing my own inner work and healing:

1. I am a good person even when other people don't think so.
2. When I take care of my needs, everybody wins.
3. Nobody, I repeat, nobody needs to be saved or rescued, including Mother Earth.

As I implemented these three principles powerfully in my life, everything transformed. I trusted myself to say no and I liked the reasons why I was saying no. How I felt by the end of the night mattered to me because I finally mattered to me. How I treated those most sacred in my life by the end of the day mattered to me because our interactions mattered, THEY mattered and I was tired of giving the resentment scraps. How I showed up in the world became my own vision of how I wanted to show up - not my parents' vision, or the church's vision or the other moms around me or the other female entrepreneurs.

I began loving saying no, even when the other person was outwardly or secretly appalled by it. I welcomed the practice of having my own back when Lucy kicked in telling me that I was being "bad". For the first time in my lif- I wasn't lying to myself anymore and pretending to be something that I wasn't or giving what I did not have. I also trusted that those people around me were capable of figuring things out. I discovered that when I want to save or rescue anyone, I am ignoring my own work and I am leaving an opportunity on the table for growth.

I was finally creating my own dream - my own vision for my life and it felt good.

You're always doing one of three things:

> **1. Expecting others to behave in a certain way in order to bring you happiness; other people expect you to behave in a certain way to bring them happiness.** If you wanted to stay this way, you would not be reading this book. You would be running in the other direction. This state, however, is the natural survival state. It was what we were raised with. Be good, Don't Rock the Boat and you will not be punished either physically, or psychologically.
>
> The fear of abandonment is one of the huge shadow

pillars that we experience in our life. It's the reason I work with my clients to cultivate greater levels of self-integrity. When you understand yourself and are willing to have your own back through all of the emotions that you experience, you grow stronger in your conviction of how you want to live your life. It's okay to admit that the childhood that you had is not the one that you want to continue living in. And that those old patterns of survival that kept you flying under the radar in your life are no longer working as an adult. Your parents can be both great people and wounded individuals. This work is so important because the methods that were used on you as a child are what you are unknowingly doing to yourself - and to others.

THIS causes chaos. It's the reason that blowups happen with no change in behavior. It is the reason you can live with people for decades and be disconnected from them.

When you grow tired of the chaos, you begin moving on to step 2. It's in this space that you realize how much trying to change someone else's behavior DRAINS you (and only creates more disconnect).

2. Rewriting your relationship manual so that you change the way that you think about other people's behavior. in this space, you're only working on you and you are not expecting the other person to change their behavior at all.

The answer to your long-lasting positive transformation resides in your desire for something different and knowing that all of the people outside of you are not going to be the ones to change first.

If you want change in your life, you will have to become the person that has that result. From within.

I think that was the hardest realization to come to terms with because it was so much easier to say, "Okay, this is what needs to change, then list all of the ways that they are behaving like selfish assholes." It was easier not to consider that there were patterns coming from within me that set these interactions into motion. My commitment to becoming aware of my role in the equation and healing it through my own awareness completely changed the game - it's where I took full 100% control over my life. I could then be really honest with myself and choose to NOT be in that pattern.

Know Thyself.

When you do - you create clarity for you and that changes the trajectory of how any communication goes. It's understanding how you step into and play with the drama triangle - with others and with yourself. It's going through the five Windows exercise to overcome using that Lucy energy to communicate.

You step into clarity first instead of trying to solve a disagreement from emotional pain. Your clarity resides in your willingness to get yourself out of the drama triangle instead of relying on your interaction with another person to do so.

Your awareness of the patterns is the beginning because up until that point, they are like Velcro. Constantly stuck to you and used in all interactions. They're automatic. You don't even question your first reaction - anger or defensiveness or sadness or guilt (the victim reaction) or the villain reaction (attacking, righteous behavior, shaming, rejecting) because that's all you have known.

Your desire for something different is what fuels transformation. Your desire causes you to make a powerful decision to commit to change. That's growth.

When you commit to your own growth and you commit to inner healing, what you are saying to yourself is, "I'm tired of the bullshit, I've tried to make everyone happy and nothing is working. My life sucks and this needs to stop!"

During that process, you'll meet parts of yourself that you never really knew existed, you'll feel feelings that in the past you would have run away from, you'll begin to listen to them without believing them. You'll heal the intense emotions by yourself and commit to being the person that you've always needed.

Your own BFF. Your own wise and loving parent. The person that nurtures as well as lovingly kicks you in the ass when you need it, without the dosing of judgment and shame.

I'll give you a great example of rewriting your relationship manuals. My middle son is a complete and total pig in his room. I mean, it is a royal mess - from clothes on the floor to cups of water everywhere to potato chip bags not thrown away. For a long time, we argued and argued. I was viewing his messiness as disrespect. And being in that perspective caused me to show up like a tyrant. Now, everybody in my family is strong-willed. I got tired of constantly fighting with him. So I decided to begin reviewing the situation with a new lens.

What I wanted to make sure of was that the common areas stayed neat and tidy. I decided to let go of my own inner need to have his room cleaned along with the stories that I was telling myself about why he was so messy. That story was a childhood narrative. My father wanted every part of the house to be tidy as a mark of respect towards him. It was in this space that I never knew boundaries. My room was a reflection of that - my space was the way that he wanted. That thought process bled into all parts of my life. As I began my own quest to set and maintain better boundaries, I inventoried where I was encroaching on other people's. It was in that space that I was able to rewrite the meaning in MY mind.

My story did not have to be my father's. My son's unwillingness to have a tidy space did not have to mean anything except that - he did not have a problem with it.

Basically, I stopped making it about me. I decided that I have a finite amount of time left with him in this household and that I did not want to meet him everyday in a space of conditional love, meaning that I would be nice to him if he did exactly as I asked.

Something really great happened, as I began internally making this shift. No, he did not magically become this super tidy person, but when I did ask him to pick up his room every couple of weeks in an energy that was not tyrannical and berating, he did it on the first ask. There were even times where he cleaned his room completely on his own (gasp, I know!).

How I responded to him and chose to interact with him created the desired result because it was not happening out of authoritarianism and fear.

It's not expecting him to be anything different. It is the internal work of shifting the perspective and not being so narcissistic about people's behavior toward you. You can create magic in your life and relationships simply by healing yourself and allowing yourself the opportunity to change the meaning that you are assigning to another person's behavior.

3. Setting clear and distinct boundaries - identifying behaviors that are clearly not working. Behaviors ranging from shaming, blaming, guilt, anger and manipulation. It is in the space that there is a consequence to the lack of behavioral change.

Most people will tell you that they struggle with this one. That it is so hard. When you tell yourself that it's so hard, that is your Lucy speaking. It's not hard when you have your own back. It's not hard when you understand exactly why you are setting a boundary.

One of the things I detest is lying. When I refused to set boundaries, I was lying to myself. I was lying to my relationships. I was eroding the very foundation of Truth and unconditional love that I was so thirsty to create and experience in my life.

∼

I believe in my own resiliency and I believe in the durability of my relationships. I believe powerfully that my relationships want Growth and Truth.

∼

THAT is my Soul's due north.

When I'm honest with myself and my bandwidth, I put myself in a position to joyfully serve in Truth instead of sacrificing myself on the bed of codependency.

Many times, we struggle with the idea of saying no as if it makes us the worst person in the world. Like we are responsible for making sure that the other person's needs are met at the expense of our own well-being. What I started to really understand in the whole boundary setting process is that my No's are the kindest act of growth for the other person as well. Our relationships, if we could see them energetically, would look like a giant spider web connecting us and them at so many parts of our body.

Oftentimes we think that codependency means massively abusive relationships, yet it is not just that. Whenever we think that someone SHOULD do something for us to keep us happy or vice versa, that is codependency. The idea that we are in a relationship in order to create emotional happiness is one of the most damaging concepts to our growth and to theirs.

We were raised by people that weren't doing the inner work. We were taught conditional behavior. If I make you happy, then I'm a good person. If I don't, then I'm not. The inner work allows us to unlearn all of that. Personal responsibility creates personal autonomy. It creates the sovereignty that we've been craving.

We think that we have been craving happiness; however, what we are really craving is the ability to feel centered no matter what. No matter what emotion we experience, we can always find our way back to our own center. When I began this work, I asked myself how I wanted to feel most of the time. That pointed me to what I needed to cut out. In the process of cutting things out I was going to ignite intense negative emotions to navigate and field during that process to create more levels of column in my life.

What I knew deep in my bones was that I was willing to experience all of it to create the kind of life, relationships and business that I wanted to experience on a regular basis. I stopped requiring other people around me to be good with my choices.

You get to decide to be the governor of your energy, to decide powerfully where the energy is focused and be super fucking unapologetic about it. And to give no explanation for your reasoning. I'm seeing that a lot lately - expressing personal autonomy and then being asked by somebody else to defend my reasoning behind it. The exciting part is that all of these experiences allow me to simply root even deeper into my own centeredness, my own resiliency and to amplify my own inner safety.

When I am centered in my big cojone heart and say no, I am being unapologetically truthful to myself and I'm being transparent in my relationships. That is a level of honesty that I want to reciprocate in my relationships. True give and take.

My saying no builds independence; my saying no builds resilience. My saying no builds competency; my saying no builds resourcefulness in the other person. It not only does it for us, guys, yet our default brain struggles with whether or not we're selfish. I would invite you to allow yourself to sink into this thing that is the kindest, most loving thing that you can do for yourself. But also... saying no, and practicing healthy boundaries, is the kindest and most loving thing that you can do for the other person.

When you begin setting boundaries in your life, your inner people pleaser - the wounded child - will fire up. This is the fire left within you telling you that you are bad, that you should feel guilty, and you are definitely mean for wanting to tolerate less emotional s*** in your life.

Here's the thing, though; you are making agreements to tolerate less of your own shit. Everything is a pattern. Every interaction that we experience is merely a reflection of the patterns that are firing with us.

It's part of the reason why inner work is so vital. You have to be willing to have your own back when other people push their agenda on you. It's deciding powerfully that your patterns are no longer working in your life. It's deciding powerfully that your patterns are damaging yourself and others more than benefiting everyone.

Making a decision to no longer keep the peace is freedom for everyone involved. Our biggest hurdle is continually dropping back into that wounded child energy and forgetting the agreements that we have made with our self to grow and mature our wounds, turning them into wisdom. These are some of my favorite questions that I ask myself when saying no:

 What do they want from me and do I WANT to give it?

Not can I - of course I can - I am someone that manages MANY things at once. This is precisely what caused my immune system to crash. Now, it's do I want to, because then I can be really honest with myself. If I say yes, I know that I am doing so from a place of joyful service.

 Are there shoulds, woulds and coulds coming up?

If there are, then I can reassure my Lucy that I am not responsible for this. Then go back to question 1.

 How am I taking responsibility for this, why and whose responsibility is it?

When the shoulds, woulds and coulds come up, that usually means that Lucy is trying to people please and overachieve. Gently soothe her and go back to question 1.

 If I feel bad, it's just an opportunity to do my inner work.

Five Windows exercise, here I come. Then go back to question 1.

How will we all grow by me saying no?

Make yourself answer this question beyond, "I don't know," otherwise you'll focus on Lucy and the wounds that want to get praise, worth and value from someone else.

We have all been in and will fall back into expecting each other to create happiness. Whenever we get triggered, it is because number one is being poked and prodded. It's in this space that you can practice your DUHS - decide to say no (love your reason because you matter) and then understand that it will feel icky, and have your own back through reassurance, which allows you to soothe yourself.

You grow stronger. Your sense of Self becomes stronger. And others will begin to understand that you matter because you finally believe it from within.

As you believe that you matter deep from within, saying no becomes easy.

Back in 2011, my back was against a wall and I had some important decisions to begin making in my life. I was spreading myself too thin and could no longer afford to do so. A big part of my inner work was learning how to begin setting and implementing boundaries. As a people pleaser, it was some of the most intense inner work of my life. Out of that work though, core values were built and adhered to.

My due north was:

Family.

Sufficiency.

Calm.

Joy.

And I begin building my life and making my decisions around those core values.

Have a client come to me that only wants to work on Saturdays? *Nope.*

Have family demand my presence and it clearly won't be welcomed? *Nope.*

Have someone ask a "favor" of me that will likely drain my energy? *Nope.*

Have someone ask me to volunteer when I know that it's not a good fit? *Nope.*

Taking a phone call when I know that my energy is already low? *Nope.*

I DO ask myself if it feels fun - for me too.

I DO ask myself how I will show up at home later on - because expending my energy in the name of family and then treating my family like crap is not service.

I DO ask myself if I am in a place to say yes joyfully - because isn't that the energy that I want to bring instead of grumbly resentment?

I am willing to leave money on the table in honor of these core values.

I am willing to let go of relationships in honor of these core values.

I am willing to look like an ass in the eyes of someone else in honor of these core values.

People will tell you that you shouldn't think that way, that it is selfish of you. I call big ol' bullshit. You matter. Your energy matters. Where you want to focus it... matters.

When you understand your core values and live by them unapologetically, saying no becomes easy. And everyone wins.

You can begin to do the inner work that leaves the baggage in the past and takes the lessons and gifts with you. Be LESS of a bitch by saying no more often.

Go Beyond the White Picket Fence

Download the Free Workbook here:

https://gromen.lpages.co/beyond-the-white-picket-fence-workbook/

In the next chapter...

My boundaries don't protect me or anyone else.

They are success standards that I have in place that allow me to take care of myself and ensure that I am giving my best to everybody else. This way I don't fall back into the old habit of self-sacrifice and then resenting everyone around me for not taking care of me. It is that belief system that erodes my own self trust and worthiness - it also erodes the integrity of the relationship that I have with myself and other people.

These parameters are teachers, giving all of us an opportunity to understand how doing and being go hand-in-hand. How to be honest and clear with myself, so that I can be honest and clear with everyone around me. When I model this, miracles happen – and those around me begin to model this behavior as well. Relationships feel two- sided instead of one person always giving and the other taking, which is just exhausting.

When I am holding my boundaries, I'm taking responsibility for my own growth and how I want to direct my energy. Boundaries and personal parameters are not weapons. They are tools for growth. They are healing the past wounds so that I no longer use the pain from my childhood to create chaos in my life now.

THIS is what I help my clients re-discover ... the centeredness and harmony that exists within their life and business when they heal the barriers of the beliefs that make them think that personal parameters are bad.

They are not. They are life giving.

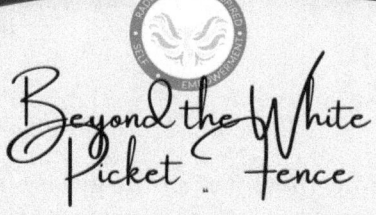

Your future is transformed by your willingness to heal your past. When you perceive your past in a new light, you can re-write your present and create more goodness in your life.

PEDESTALS AND CROSSES

Once upon a time, there was a little girl who was constantly told that she was NOTHING like her mother and just like her father. She thought that made her bad, yet there was no way she would ever be like her mother Was being like her father so bad? So, for a long time - she wore armor to protect herself from others' opinions. She didn't realize that she also kept love from herself.

She healed and re-wrote her story. As she did, she learned to love all of herself even when others wished that she was someone else.

For the longest time, I simultaneously wanted to be just like my parents and nothing like my parents. That was the biggest conundrum, because in order to begin living more fully like myself, I had to come to terms with the fact that I had baggage. I had to be willing to stop running from it. It was hard to admit that I had been creating a life that looked awesome on the outside but that felt exactly like my childhood on the inside.

I was mimicking my parents - the parts I swore I would never become. It wasn't until I decided that it was no longer working for me (or my life and family) that I was willing to begin facing myself instead of continuing to place blame on my parents for being the people that they were. It's in the space that I stopped making excuses for why I behaved the way I did and made a commitment to become more responsible for my own emotional nourishment and well-being.

I had to be willing to take my parents off the pedestal (and off the cross). I had to begin understanding that they were people with wounds instead of the superheroes that I wanted them to be. I needed to forgive myself for holding onto an ideal instead of processing and navigating the baggage of my past so that it would stop impacting my current reality.

My past was showing up in all parts of my life. From being afraid to move forward in my own business to making my husband and kids look after me emotionally, I had zero coping skills for my intense emotions and for a very long time, I made excuses for things like blowups and meltdowns like they were out of my control.

When I became a full-grown adult, it was completely in my control to embark on a journey of self-discovery and learn coping skills that would help me understand my wounds better so that they stopped creating chaos in my life today. So that I could create a better partnership with my husband. So that I could understand myself so powerfully and re-parent myself, allowing my communications with my kids to be less muddy.

The first level of my journey began when my oldest son became a teenager and I saw the patterns that were mimicking from my own childhood. I had a deep desire to have a better relationship with him than I had growing up. I got tired of my excuses like, "Well, it's just because he's a teenager," As if our fighting had nothing to do with me and everything to do with him. It simply wasn't true and embarking on wanting to become more fully myself and have a better relationship with him meant that I had to be willing to look at the modeling that I had in my past.

And I had to begin holding my Lucy accountable, healing her and no longer have her swirling and creating havoc in my life and relationships. To be the parent that I needed to myself now and then wife and parent from a space of emotional fullness instead of emotional deficiency.

In order to become more fully you, you have to understand that you do want something different from your parents, a different flavor if you will. You want a life done your way. And that is okay. With this realization, you will come to terms with the fact that what you want moving forward is different from what your parents modeled for you. That realization can bring on a lot of anger and guilt though, like we are being bad little kids and not appreciating what they gave us. Or as if we want to leave the past in the past hoping that whatever happened will never surface again.

One of our biggest hurdles for healing our internal trauma is our refusal to acknowledge that our parents actually did something wrong in the way that they parented or that what they did is negatively impacting us today in ways that we do not see, but we certainly feel.

The need to keep them on the pedestal or the cross usually happens because we feel betrayal - of ourselves, our ideals, of them. And healing takes the energy away that we have been using errantly in our life to feel safer.

It's not easy to feel your emotional pain, on purpose, to be willing to see how it's been creating in your life. I know that I found it hard.

After my dad died, I ran from that emotional pain for seven months before I finally hit a level of rock bottom. I was so angry at him for being unwilling to change his behaviors - physically, mentally and emotionally. I felt such guilt that my love simply did not seem enough. He died alone and I beat myself up for that for the longest time.

I felt betrayed on so many levels, being made to be more responsible at a young age, navigating sexual predators and abusers at a young age, having no voice to say anything and when I did speak, I was labeled difficult.

And yet, I still deeply loved my parents. Which just pissed me off even more.

I wanted so badly for my father to not be an addict, to love me the way I needed to be loved and a lot of my childhood was me trying to figure out who to be in order for him to see ME instead of expecting me to be something that I was not. And because I did not know that I could begin giving this to myself, this pattern of looking outside for love played out in my life for decades.

From boyfriends, to bosses, to friends and mentors, I looked outside of myself for love, praise and accolades. To locate it from within meant that I had to take a look at the baggage, the pain and be willing to finally release it. When I did though, that was the freedom that I needed and craved so deeply.

At the core, I was looking for acceptance. from him instead of finally giving it to myself. It also was the one thing that I was not giving him because I could not give it to myself.

Here is one of the biggest gateways to healing - duality. You can love them AND acknowledge that they left you with some baggage that has to be healed from within so that your life can flourish and thrive versus simply being another generation of people perpetuating negative patterns.

Our parents didn't know it all. They also did the best that they could. That doesn't mean that we don't have some negative patterns to unravel. We do.

Throughout our childhood we uphold them as the utmost authority in our life. Now that we are adults and we are beginning to acknowledge our own internal chaos, there is this cognitive dissonance within us. They parented from their wounds and now we have some clean up to do, and we still might feel badly about wanting that healing for ourselves because of what we are admitting.

Some people might call it being broken. I don't think that at all. I think of it as calling fragments home for healing through acceptance and forgiveness for keeping them in the dark for so long.

There is large trauma and then there are these little microtraumas that shape our behavior within childhood. It gives us a pathway of "safety". For example, when my mom gets overwhelmed, my Lucy will have this need to be super helpful. When my dad began yelling, my Lucy felt the need to go to my room and just be quiet and stay under the radar. Those are old childhood patterns, which can show up today by anticipating others needs and over-doing to mitigate drama or procrastinating having hard conversations for fear of someone's reaction. Trauma is not just basic needs being met or not. It's the large and small events in our life that condition our reaction to other people and outside events.

Some of the beliefs that shaped how I showed up as an adult stemmed from these phrases in my childhood:

- Children should be seen and not heard.
- Stop crying before I give you something to cry about.
- I'm so disappointed in you.
- You're making me look bad.
- Act like a big girl.

Yes, for most of my life, my basic needs were met. I most definitely had been carrying around emotional pain though through the vehicles of shame and fear. What I was raised with became my internal critical voice - and THAT I can heal.

I call it the "white picket fence" silent pain, the pain that we carry from childhood. The pain that no one knows that we carry. The feelings of emptiness or disconnection - from ourself and from our family. The ways that we escape or hide from our fears. The continual people pleasing so we do not feel rejected in our lives and relationships.

I had hopes for something different and this deep internal need to present to everyone like I had it all together at all times.

We don't talk about the pain because maybe we don't even know that it's our childhood trauma that's responsible for the chaos in our adult life. The anxiety that we feel is us trying to keep a lid on that box so that no one can see our pain and use it against us and because up until this point, we have not known how to show up for it ourself and navigate it in a way that is healthy.

It shows up in adulthood as failed relationships, abusive relationships, depression, overwhelm, the need to constantly please, the need to constantly control, the need to save, overworking, high achieving, perfectionism, exhaustion and even full on physical disease. There's a long list.

Because on the outside, to other people, your life and family appeared perfect.

And inside the four walls of your childhood home, there was behavior that conditioned you to expect the other shoe to most definitely drop.

- Growing up in addiction.
- Growing up with verbal, emotional, mental and/or sexual abuse.
- Witnessing volatility.
- Witnessing infidelity.
- Witnessing manipulation.
- Being forced to grow up and be responsible at a very young age - even taking care of the adults that were supposed to take care of you.
- Being provided for yet not getting the nurturing and nourishment that you needed as a child.
- Being surrounded in emotional unavailability.

ALL of the experiences in your childhood have created your Lucy and the experiences that you have in your adult life today are just a series of reactions from old experiences that keep on cycling in your life.

With the various exercises in this book as well as the free offerings that you can sign up for, you begin to understand how she reacts in your adult life and you begin to create awareness around what triggers those reactions. In this way you can begin to take 100% responsibility for them.

Other people do not cause us to get upset. We think that they are; however, that is not the case.

No one can really hurt your feelings - only your own thoughts and feelings about yourself, the person and the situation can. Your own nervous system that fires can. The part of us that has not healed and gleaned the wisdom from the experiences does.

That is great news because, with awareness and commitment to unlearning these patterns, you gain control of your reactions, heal them and step into the choice of responding, which is fueled with wisdom and discernment.

It's where calm is created in your life and relationships - ON PURPOSE.

It's where YOU take the wheel of your own life.

Not Jesus. Not the Universe. And definitely not Lucy.

You begin to outgrow your victim self and your villain self. You live beyond the drama triangle. The hero of your story begins to get a new definition.

You move from surviving in your life, dodging the moment-to-moment chaos, and you begin to navigate the emotional waters with ease, flow and greater levels of control.

Understanding what you needed as a child and begin to give yourself that now.

Do it daily. Unapologetically. As you make it your practice, you will advocate for those around you to do the same. You can model it for others.

The five love languages, prioritizing yourself, understanding and creating awareness around your Lucy gives you the opportunity to re-parent yourself, to set clear boundaries and re-shape the quality of your relationships. You can give yourself the love, emotional nourishment, acceptance and forgiveness instead of waiting for others (who are wounded people too) to give it to you.

What feeling would you like to experience more of in your life? Create it from within.

What feeling do you know that you want? Give it to yourself, stop putting yourself last and then waiting for others to pick up your emotional pieces. That is YOU beginning to take 100% responsibility for healing your Lucy and taking her out of the driver's seat in your life.

What habits are working against you? Becoming aware and holding yourself accountable in a new way creates new outcomes.

It's where YOU take control over your emotional well-being and stop expecting others to give you what you can, as an adult, give to yourself. In this space, you have your own back.

You move yourself from chaos to calm, on purpose, no matter what. That is true empowerment. With this new practice, you help model and build something new around you. You begin to break the chains of codependency.

You create inner freedom.

What are the gifts of your past?

You cannot change the past. However, you can transform how you perceive your past and re-write your present.

You cannot change what the experiences were or how other people acted. You can, however, acknowledge who you have become as a result of your past - what gifts did you cultivate as a result of your upbringing?

Too many people focus on wishing that they could change their past because of how it's negatively impacting their present life and their future. Your past is your past and yes, it includes pain. It also includes opportunities for you to be more intuitive, resourceful, adaptable, insightful.

I'll give you an example:

> *As a result of my past, I have learned how to trust my feelings implicitly. I have learned that my honesty and my clarity is a gift even when other people don't see it. I have learned how to*

hone my radar for safety and I have learned how to trust my intuition implicitly.

I'm a great leader.

I know that my love and my ability to accept reality as it is gives me powerful Clarity and wisdom.

None of those skills would have been honed had I had a different childhood.

Until I did my healing work, I wished for another childhood. That's how I created the white picket fence life where I was hiding my gifts underneath the emotional pain that I was trying to bury.

In order for these gifts to be recovered, I had to be willing to allow myself to feel pissed about my past, to be sad about my past, to acknowledge how I have been running from myself because I wanted to forget that my past even existed. For the longest time I saw that my past made me weak.

What I realized was that what made me the weakest was running away from those parts of me that were wounded. It's in recovering those wounds and healing them that made me who I am today.

I am a woman who sees her tumultuous past as the biggest gift in her life. I am a woman who can speak her truth from a place of self-awareness, self-integrity, Clarity and wisdom. I am a woman who accepts others for who they are and is always willing to set a boundary for self-preservation - no matter who that person is. I am a woman who embodies and communicates from honor, respect, and appreciation. I am a woman who will always be honest and vulnerable with herself - because she knows that is the foundation for self-integrity and clarity, which produces calm, connected, sustainable relationships.

What are the gifts of your past and who have you become as a result?

∼

Forgiveness and Acceptance.

∼

I think that forgiveness is really us freeing ourselves and other people from expectations of being someone that they simply are not capable of being. Not everyone is interested in self-improvement. Accepting them where they are gives me a great opportunity to give what I was needing to myself, to accept myself fully and forgive that part of me that wants to wait around for someone to give me something that I can now give to myself, through my own healing.

All of us are shaped through our experiences and perspectives. Who I think somebody should be and the reality of who they are can produce two very different perspectives, especially if I am forgetting that my lovability and my worth are within.

I forgive myself as an act of love to myself (my wounded Lucy), acknowledging that this pattern is a wound and it has been creating chaos in my life while I've been waiting for someone to be something that they are not.

It doesn't mean that I absolve other people of their behavior or release them from being responsible for their actions. Forgiveness does not mean that the trauma I experienced as a child is my fault, it's not. I forgive because I want to release those parts of pain that I have been holding on to and bring those fragments home to my heart for healing.

This work has allowed me to free myself and set better boundaries because I have my own back. Shame and fear have zero hold when you are willing to bring the fragments home for healing from within instead of waiting for someone else to meet an expectation.

I wrote this letter to my mom a few years ago. See, while I talk about my father and how difficult he was, that does not mean that I didn't have work to do with my mother too. I did. I carried quite a bit of rage towards my childhood experiences. The inner work has allowed me to heal those parts, feel safer from within, forgive and accept. That has allowed me to see through the eyes of beauty and wisdom instead of through the eyes of emotional pain.

Dear Mom,

When I was young, I wanted to be EXACTLY like you. You walked around with grace and beauty. Everyone loved you. You smiled. Boy, oh boy, you smiled and that smile lit up the whole room. What I now know is that the smile was the outward expression of your light and THAT is what lit up the room. How grateful I am that I got to and get to witness that light everyday.

I wanted that. I wanted to be able to hold that kind of light. I couldn't wait to be older so that I could be just like you.

When I was a little older, I no longer wanted to be just like you. I saw all of the mistakes that you made. I blamed you for making them. I only saw the hurt that I experienced from those choices, never thinking about how they also impacted you. I looked at your decisions as weak and being taken advantage of. I saw your kindness and compassion as prey for the predators of life.

I swore that I would never be like you.

And then life started happening.

And little by little I started learning the whats, the wheres, the hows, the whys to your journey. I grew compassion for every part of your journey. I grew to love every part of you. I grew in forgiveness – to you, to me – to us – to life. I grew to desire to be like you again.

But not just like you. Because I am me. And it took me a long time to understand that. So I took your grace and wove it into my life. Grace that accepted life as it is. Grace that saw the beauty in the mistakes. Grace that was forged through the strength and resilience of life dealings. As it turns out, strength and resilience aren't realized in our moments of weakness, they are realized when we come out on the other side of darkness. You have shown me what grace through strength and resilience looked like.

The situations in my life that forged that kind of resilience looked NOTHING like yours, but when I needed to be reminded what grace through strength and resilience looked like, I had those moments and your example to turn to. Thank you.

And I took your beauty, your view of beauty and wove it into my life. I stopped to honor the small things. Those things that you KNOW you might forget in the long run, but that I just might remember because I stopped to see the beauty, but even if you don't remember in the long term – you took the time to pause in the moment now. You showed me what it was like to see beauty in every situation. "How can we make the best of it?" or "What is the silver lining?" are my go to questions now. Because of you and your journey – I am reminded that beauty is everywhere and as life happens, I can always find the silver lining.

The silver linings in my life have looked NOTHING like the silver linings in yours, and I am reminded that they never had to. The lesson of beauty all around is cemented in. Thank you.

I took that warmth of your smile and wove it into my life. That smile that said "I see you" to everyone that you meet. I didn't fully understand that "smile at everyone" part of you when I was younger. As I got older, I realized that the smile really meant, "Yes, I see you, I know that you have seen pain and joy and love and loss. Me too. I see you. We are here." That smile permeated every part of whoever you met. I understand now that your smile delivered compassion and warmth to everyone because we are human and sharing warmth is establishing connection.

My ways of sharing warmth and establishing connection look NOTHING like the ways that yours did, but because of your example – I know and feel what that looks like. Because you shared your smile with me, the one that says, "I see you," I was able to develop that warmth within me and share it with everyone that I meet. Thank you.

I was and still am honored to be in the presence of your light. At first, I was scared of it thinking that I would never be able to be THAT kind of light. But then I realized that what you were showing me was how to shine – not to shine just like you – and that is a HUGE difference.

When you walk in, the room lights up – some people like it, others do not. You showed me that shining anyway was the key to life.

Funny thing, my way of shining looks NOTHING like yours, but it shares that warmth and zest that you have too. You showed me that it was more than okay, that it was essential to shine your light, because everyone benefits when you shine your light.

And that there is no set way to shine your light.

Shine.

And you did, you do, and you empower me to keep doing the same. Thank you.

A million times over, thank you. I love you always.

The freedom that you wish to feel from within resides in your willingness to heal the parts that have been hidden, acceptance and forgiveness is the superhighway that will get you there.

Other people and their opinions will always be there - shine anyways.

Go Beyond the White Picket Fence

Download the free workbook to access one of my FAVORITE forgiveness exercises.

https://gromen.lpages.co/beyond-the-white-picket-fence-workbook/

In the next chapter...

At some point in time in your life you will say to yourself, "No more". And instead of blowing up, dropping out and then shaming yourself for hitting your limit only to do it all again in a few days - you'll begin to make small changes.

This happens when you stop avoiding the emotional reaction that you've been afraid of experiencing.

Of feeling the shame that comes with being told that you suck. Or that you are the meanest person ever. Or that you are ... selfish.

Avoiding the shame, the anger and the guilt only keeps you in an emotional YES. And it keeps everyone from growing.

See, their opinions might be true at the moment for them, but when YOU decide that it has no impact on you, you step into the field of growth. Then you begin to take back your power and build safety from within, which produces MASSIVE inner strength. .

You will finally be part of what you consider when you are making decisions and rebuilding your relationships. You'll begin to ask yourself what is good for you by really getting honest with what's no longer working.

You will begin to heal. You'll begin to intentionally create your day factoring yourself into it. You'll no longer be a servant to your life.

And that is when you enter the gateway of calmer, more energized living.

Others may call you "difficult" - I call you the ULTIMATE caretaker of your own energy.

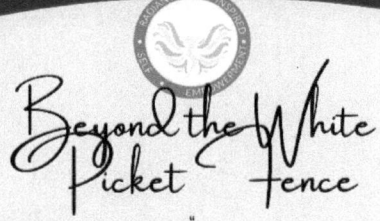

"Let them come with all of their opinions. I guarantee, when you decide powerfully to have your own back and embark on your own Self discovery journey, you will use your interactions as a growth exercise to propel you even further into your healing instead of hiding who you are.

Your healing IS the ultimate gift to your world.

AFTERWORD
WINNING AT (RE)PARENTING.

Once upon a time there was a young woman who got all dolled up for a party. When she arrived, she was met with blank stares and side eyes from other women, which made her believe that something was "wrong" with her. Wanting to fit in, she found herself performing instead of just being herself. As she grew and healed, she realized that as long as she loved her light from within, those stares and side eyes had no impact on her. As a matter of fact … she enjoyed being herself - no matter what.

You will have to decide over and over again to make a decision that works for you, as the adult in your life. You will make these decisions and then meet everyone else's opinions on it, giving you an opportunity to root into your wise Self even more.

It's beautiful.

AFTERWORD

And sometimes that will feel daunting and hard. As you keep your conviction, commitment and intentional movement, it becomes easier. You get more willing to see your own shit and heal it instead of spinning yourself in overwhelm, exhaustion and guilt even more.

Recently, I made a decision to outsource my laundry. And it brought up all sorts of drama. I knew that I needed help and I rolled around with a ton of thoughts and feelings about what that made me (this woman that no longer wanted to do laundry).

Bougie.
Selfish.
High Maintenance.
Wrong.
Not a good mother.

As a stay-at-home mom for most of my life, aren't I just supposed to suck it up and do it? Well, no. Now, hear me on this because if I was still a SAHM and no longer wanted to do laundry, I would make the same choice that I am now.

Currently, I own myself as a powerful woman. A woman who runs businesses and moms and wants to enjoy life even more.

It was meeting with MY coach that helped me really get to the root of what was keeping me from making a decision to finally do something that would bring my life more ease. What I found was that I was really scared of two things - trusting someone with intimate parts of myself and whether or not I wanted a "new" person in my home, and what identity I was afraid of releasing.

AFTERWORD

This identity was being that woman who is doing it all at the peril of her well-being. She is unhealthy and spinning in a narrative that she is useful and relevant when she does it all. Whew - that was under the radar and churning all of the anxiety.

I was scared to enjoy my success, to admit that this was not a task that I wanted to do anymore and to begin the process (and stay committed to) of finding a solution that works for me.

I DID find a solution that night. When you decide powerfully to commit to change, the energy will conspire to help you so things taking time is, well - a narrative.

I had to begin thinking and feeling a new way while I created something new. Here are the new thoughts that I began having about myself:

I AM a powerful woman who hires help in all areas of her life to create enjoyment and ease.
I AM a woman who is relevant because I am.
I AM willing and ready to create a life with ease, pleasure and leisure.
I AM a woman who has FUN in life and in business.
I AM a woman who has durable relationships.
I AM a woman that frees herself from being responsible of making other people happy.
I AM a woman who easily lets go of other people's opinions.

Now, guess what? I hired a laundry service and excitedly told some people in my life. They gave me ALL of their opinions on why that was certainly a bad idea. I heard "Why do YOU need to have your laundry done?", "Aren't you scared that they will lose it?", "I would NEVER do that.", "You are okay with someone

AFTERWORD

touching your laundry? Gross." These comments were from people that I am close to and love.

I found myself saying this.

 We have different opinions on this. I am really excited about the freedom in time that I will have.

Simple, right?

Yes. And I was left with my own inner work of soothing my Lucy that maybe wanted to agree with all those thoughts.

Their thoughts are yours ONLY if you agree with them. And if you do, then do your inner work while you head towards what you want to create.

Appreciate what you have and CREATE what you want - unapologetically. Feel what it would feel like NOW to have that result, even through all of the drama that Lucy will try to give you. That is really the magic formula for transforming your life.

Reparent yourself first. Then model that for everyone around you.

That is the ripple.

I went to cryotherapy yesterday and was complimented on the behavior of my oldest son. The lady at the counter told me that every time he comes in he is so polite and respectful and that she just doesn't see that from many twenty-year-olds.

I smiled and thanked her and told her that out of everything that I have done in my life that I really feel like I'm winning at parenting.

AFTERWORD

I'm pretty sure that she was simply expecting me to say thank you and move on. Her face said so and it gave me an opportunity to do my own inner work because there was part of me that felt a lot of shame for saying that statement out loud, for celebrating very openly that I feel like I have "won" parenting.

After really sitting with myself and soothing myself, I stand behind my statement. Not because parenting is easy or that my kids are unicorns. Life is still happening. There are many times where I facepalm - over myself, over them, over choices or directions. There are times where they are not at their best and nor am I. Parenting is fucking hard and it's the best. Having a loving partnership is work and it is the best.

Self-accountability is EFFORT and it is the best.

The pathway of inner healing is worth the discomfort on so many levels. I feel like I have hit the lottery over and over again when I have awareness of my Lucy and make a healthier choice in how I perceive and respond to life.

I feel like I'm winning at parenting because I have actively gone on a journey to re-parent myself And that has changed the quality of every single relationship that I have. I understand my own wounds and no longer allow Lucy to be the driver in my life.

I don't expect my kids or husband to emotionally pick me up in ways that are unhealthy for all of us. And they don't expect it either. That is a win on so many levels.

I understand my own fears and that allows me to get out of their way when my kids do something that pokes at that fear or my husband does something that rubs my abandonment wound. It gives me an opportunity to model for them how to empower

AFTERWORD

themselves, to set boundaries in their own lives and show up in a way that feels empowered for them.

I can hold space for them when they are upset without making it mean anything, without having to solve for it, without having this deep desire to save and rescue them out of these deep and painful emotions. I have learned how to navigate my own deep waters of intense emotions and not be afraid of them and that ensures that I am not afraid of anyone else's either.

I no longer try to "fix" my life and my relationships from my past wounds. I heal and create in the present moment.

So can you.

Let your healing be the beacon for yourself. Let your new awareness and way of being shine in all areas of your life.

Being told that you are the devil or not "of God" is part of the process when you are stepping into greater intuitive ability. Being told that you shouldn't talk about family secrets and being shamed for doing so is part of the game when you are healing and growing.

There are so many other experiences that make us feel like we want to just back away slowly instead of being more of ourselves. Instead, go ahead and shine. It's part of growth. That uncomfortable feeling is to be celebrated. You are leaving the pack mind and stepping into being more of you fully.

They are rites of passage that give you an opportunity to meet your wounds and finally heal them - taking away the power that they've held over you. When you choose to keep going through growth, you are ultimately bringing awareness to your own darkness and shedding more light on it, it really has nothing to

AFTERWORD

do with them. Or what they think you should do or not do, or be or not be. Their opinions are not the issue; how you believe them and react has 100% to do with you having your own back through your own inner healing.

It's this, over and over again.

Let them come with all of their opinions. I guarantee, when you decide powerfully to have your own back and embark on your own self-discovery journey, you will use your interactions as a growth exercise to propel you even further into your healing instead of hiding who you are.

Your healing IS the ultimate gift to your world.

Shine.

REFERENCES

4. HEALING YOUR LUCY

1. Chapman, G. D. (2017). *The 5 love languages: The secrete to love that last.* Christian Art Publishers.

ABOUT THE AUTHOR

Tracy is a highly experienced Healer and SoulHearted Living Coach known for helping female entrepreneurs be more bold and confident in all areas of their life and business.

She specializes in teaching her clients how to make better decisions without second guessing themselves, stop taking things personally and stop feeling guilty for taking care of themselves. Instead of looking for moment to moment happiness from other people's reactions, she teaches women how to create a calmer life and business from a holistic perspective allowing all of their relationships to improve.

After suffering her own health collapse in 2011 and the re-build of health and relationships from that collapse, she leads by example and has transformed the quality of her life, family and business as a result of her own inner work.

Tracy wants to show women a different way to achieve the relationship success that they are looking for through working on themselves and allowing that inner work to transform HOW they approach their relationships, their life and their business.

She has been featured in Thrive Global, Positively Positive and Medium among other publications.

Tracy is the mom to 3 teen boys, married to her high school sweetheart and runs two successful businesses from a place of centeredness and greater calm.

You can learn more about Tracy and what she offers here:

Website: https://www.tracygromen.net/
Email: tracy@tracygromen.net
YouTube: youtube.com/channel/UCk5T0ZtB3gvNoyxN8MIeOoQ

facebook.com/Tgromen

www.ingramcontent.com/pod-product-compliance
Lightning Source LLC
Chambersburg PA
CBHW030331230426
43661CB00032B/1374/J